WHY ISN'T

Everyone

A MILLIONAIRE?

HOW OUR GOOD HABITS STOP US FROM GETTING RICHER

VALRIE CHAMBERS

ISBN: 978-1-54399-733-0 (print)

ISBN: 978-1-54399-734-7 (ebook)

This book is dedicated to Jim, Cassandra, Stephen, Clayton, Sarah, and Mavi, and to all of us who have struggled with money while feeling that we've been doing the right things financially

Acknowledgements: James Barrett, Ronny Pigg, Sarah Whitehead, Cassandra Jean Amell

CONTENTS

WHY ISN'T

Everyone

A MILLIONAIRE?

HOW OUR GOOD HABITS STOP US FROM GETTING RICHER

INTRODUCTION

We all have money habits, and those habits can help us, hurt us, or do some of both. Confusingly, some of the habits that work best when we're poor don't work well when we're richer and can actually hurt us. And, it's easy to think that other peoples' habits are bad, when those same habits make perfect sense to those of a different socioeconomic class.

For example, why do poor people spend their windfalls? Wouldn't it make more sense to save for a rainy day? Not necessarily. Here's why—first, many poor people do save, which is remarkable because we have so little left over. The biggest economic threat to us is an economic shock, like an accident with bodily injury. We can't afford the hospital bill or even the deductible if we're insured, so hospitals will take all that we have and will have to write off the rest. Now suppose we get a $500 windfall. That's huge! We can put a couple hundred aside and still have a great party or mini vacation, or we can save the whole thing.

Now, we know that crap (economic shocks) happens a lot. We don't know what will happen or when, but we do know that crap happens and when it does, it will likely wipe us out. If I save the $500, that's what I'll lose when crap happens. If I save $200 and party with $300, I'll have a party <u>and</u> lose the rest when crap happens.

The question is not, "why didn't I save it all when I had the chance?" The better question is, "why would I save any at all?" Savings do make sense to the rest of us though, because we can pay for the crap <u>and</u> invest in our future, making our futures brighter yet.

Here's another example. For most people, debt is dangerous. We fear it. If we don't repay, creditors will embarrass us and take our stuff. We may even become homeless. But now let's be rich. Face it, that's more fun. If we can usually make 10% on every dollar invested, and we can borrow money at, say 7%. That means that if we borrow $1 million, we'll make an extra $30,000 just on other peoples' money. The sole drawback to this plan is if business goes bad and we owe the 7% interest but are not making the 10%—or worse, the million is tied up, but the lender wants it back. That could wipe us out, and that's why most people think that debt is bad. But remember, we're rich, so we borrowed this money in our company's name, not our own personal name, and we've been personally taking the wealth out of the company in the form of salary, etc. So, if the lender wants the money back and we can't pay through the company, the company goes bankrupt, but the creditors don't touch our personal accounts. That is, we have the benefit of the money, but not nearly the risk of personal harm that most middle-class people do. In this world, it pays to borrow as much as we feasibly can.

These examples show that some of our money behavior isn't really irrational. A better way of looking at it is, "is this the behavior that serves us best?" Even knowing what's best isn't good enough. Money comes with feelings, and feelings—especially fear—make us do some questionable things. So, we'll take a look at our behaviors in this book, and whether they're helping or hurting us where we're currently at. We may also recognize the "crazy" behavior of our friends and relatives in this book and find that what they're doing, from their perspective, kind of works for them.

CHAPTER 1

What Is a Millionaire?

"A man with a million dollars can be as happy nowadays as though he were rich." [1]

For this book, a millionaire is someone who has accumulated at least one million U.S. dollars in net worth. A millionaire does not have to make a million dollars in income each year. Someone making less than a million per year but that has saved or inherited *net wealth* would qualify as a millionaire for purposes of this book. It is net wealth that's being measured; having a million dollars in assets is not enough to qualify if their debt is also high. Net wealth is the assets (investments and items that will be useful in the future) that we have minus the debt that we owe. A millionaire will have at least a million dollars in assets above and beyond all their debts.

For example, two neighbors have a house worth 1.2 million dollars. The first neighbor has a mortgage of $800,000 but the second neighbor has paid off their mortgage. The first neighbor would not be considered a millionaire while the second neighbor would be. This is because the first neighbor only has a net wealth of ($1.2 million – $800,000 =) $400,000, which is well shy of a million dollars in net wealth, while the second neighbor has a net worth of 1.2 million dollars because their house is paid off.

Notice in this example how both the millionaire neighbor and the indebted neighbor both live in the same neighborhood. This is common for a couple of reasons. First, as each neighbor makes more money, their ability to get credit and spend more goes up. Some neighbors spend everything they have and more (on credit) while some neighbors live beneath their means and are savers. Being a millionaire is not about flashing wealth, it's about having wealth. Many millionaires live in houses costing much less than a million, while others live large, and risk bankruptcies. While living too large can happen everywhere, it's especially visible in celebrities' lives, because they live so much of their life in the spotlight and can gain wealth more suddenly than they can gain the knowledge of how to properly manage the wealth. With the rise of social media, this visibility has increased over time.

TV Guide[2] lists actors Stephen Baldwin, Gary Busey, Randy Quaid and Burt Reynolds, and singers Tionne "T-Boz" Watkins of TLC, and Natalie Cole as celebrities that have gone broke despite promising careers. The article also notes that celebrity businessman and U.S. President Donald Trump has taken businesses bankrupt in 1991, 1992, 2004, and 2009 to re-structure or eliminate debt that the companies could not pay back. With some people, spending outpaces income, leading to financial insolvency. Boxer and celebrity Mike Tyson made more than $300 million in his career, but filed for bankruptcy in 2003, claiming an extra $23 million in debt. MC Hammer's net worth was valued at $33 million in 1991; five years later, he was bankrupt, owing $13 million in debt. Toni Braxton filed for bankruptcy in 1996, and again in 2010, having sold some of her Grammys to make ends meet.

Professional athletes face a similar problem, although having a short career should be more evident to them than to actors. MSN.com lists several professional athletes that made high salaries but went bankrupt nonetheless.[3] NFL quarterback Vince Young went bankrupt after signing a $26 million contract, in part because of legal fees. NBA's Antoine Walker earned over

$108 million but filed for bankruptcy after spending more than that on bad real estate investments, family assistance, and luxury items. WNBA and three-time Olympic gold medalist Sheryl Swoopes declared bankruptcy in 2004. Manchester United player Eric Djemba-Djemba, who made about $6.2 million, declared bankruptcy in 2007, citing poor financial planning. NHL player Jack Johnson declared bankruptcy after borrowing at high interest rates and incurring high fees after defaulting on those loans. MLB Jack Clark filed for bankruptcy in the second year of a 3-year, $8.7 million contract. His lawyer said that he "had some expensive hobbies, and I think they got ahead of him." Mike Tyson, famous in part for owning Siberian tigers, also declared bankruptcy.[4] Lawrence Taylor declared bankruptcy in 2009 due to "bad spending habits, drug addiction and poor lifestyle choices."

Sometimes people that earn large sums very quickly think that will always be the case and it isn't. We all can name people, who, for every dollar they make, they spend more, and we all can name poorer people that we know who still manage to save a little something. It is no different with celebrities. We aspire to be the millionaire, not the celebrity, or at least we don't confuse the two. The worst thing that can happen to those of us who overspend is that we win the lottery, because if we win $50 million, we may spend $60 million, and the odds that we'll win another lottery for $10 million and change our spending habits so that they're financially even are not very good. Similarly, some celebrities spend based on their current success, not their average success which included years as a starving artist. In those cases, their future is grim.

"Mo' Money, Mo' Problems:"[5] Does Everyone Want to Be a Millionaire?

Most people do, but most of us also realize that wealth is not the most important thing in life. A healthy, well-adjusted life, with a healthy, well-adjusted family and support system is worth far more, and not just because medical costs and profound problems drain wealth. Love and the smiles of our children our priceless.

About 6% of people say that they don't care about money, and another 11% say that they can live on very little.[6] There is "enough" money for some, if not most of us, when we are as financially secure as can be expected and we're willing to trade money for time with family and/or when we consider giving large sums of it away to accomplish more good in the world. However, nearly everyone wants more money.[7] And, by understanding how we move through economic classes, we may be better able to help others on a larger scale, both those who are close to us and those in society.

The premise of this book is that most of us can be millionaires, but our own thinking gets in the way—for very good reasons. The skills, habits and mindsets that allow us to survive or succeed at one socioeconomic level may actually hurt us at the next. At some level, we know the rules change, but they change gradually. Imagine Bill Gates, Warren Buffett and other billionaires sitting around a kitchen table, trading 25-cent coupons for cake mix and fabric softener. It takes imagination, because they probably do not collect coupons. Coupons like this are practical and wise at a lower-middle class level, but not at the mega-rich level of income. For billionaires, time is better spent getting a bargain on the purchase of a cake or fabric softener company or protecting their wealth through prudent tax planning. However, we also know that abandoning all we've learned because we think that the common sense rules of finance don't apply to us anymore can also be a road to financial ruin, as seen by the celebrity and athlete bankruptcy list earlier in the chapter. The trick then is to realize that the financial advice that we should be following changes some as we get wealthier. Understanding how that advice should change and accepting the changes in spite of the fear of what would have happened if we responded to changes too soon, is key.

Some of us are afraid to take risks, and those of us who take risks tend to be overly-cautious because the risk of failure looms larger than the reward of additional success.[8] For example, we might think that receiving $50 would feel just as good as receiving $100 and then losing $50. In both situations, we gain $50. We would be wrong. Most of us view a single gain of $50 *more* favorably than gaining $100 and then losing $50, even though the cash position is the same in the end. Where a loss is unsustainable, this fear makes sense, but where the loss is sustainable (as in the example above), this fear is not fully rational. Research shows that humans don't process economic information in a rational way. In fact, in 1979, two behavioral researchers, Kahneman and Tversky, presented an idea called "prospect theory," which said people valued gains and losses differently, and based their decisions on perceived gains rather than on perceived losses.

To progress to the next economic level efficiently, we need to change our thinking. We need to change our skill set but we also need to change our mindset. We must be financially skilled to properly manage wealth, but also psychologically ready to transcend to the next economic level. Sometimes our financial thinking can be off-base enough to cause psychological problems, or so a psychologist found.

Brad Klontz and his colleagues studied the money beliefs of 422 people who were seeing a therapist for money-related problems.[9] Some people stressed about having too little money, while others stressed about losing what they had. Still others felt guilty about having so much. Some disliked people with money. Some were spenders; some were savers. Klontz was able to classify people who had psychological problems with money as having one of four money "scripts:"

1. Money avoidance

2. Money worship

3. Money status

4. Money vigilance.

Members of the money avoidance group distanced themselves from money. Some believed that they did not deserve to have money; some even sabotaged their own financial well-being. Predictably, they tended to have low incomes and low net worth.

Money worshipers believed that more money would make everything better and connect their social status to what money could buy. They were often prone to compulsive hoarding, unreasonable risk-taking, workaholism and compulsive buying disorders.

Members of the money status group linked their self-worth to their net worth. They often competed to own more than those around them. They were known to take big financial risks and tell stories of big financial gains (but not losses). They saw a clear distinction between socioeconomic classes. They generally grew up poor. Other research has shown that materialism is associated with lower ratings of well-being,[10] lower levels of self-actualization, vitality and happiness, and higher levels of anxiety.[11]

Members of the money vigilance group were hesitant to share their personal information—especially their income or wealth—even with their spouse. They could be overly conservative, choosing to keep their money in a savings account with an interest rate less than the rate of inflation. They spent wisely and paid off their credit cards monthly but could be too frugal and not enjoy the benefits of what money can buy. They were sometimes overly anxious about a vague, impending financial danger.

All these groups took one of the money behaviors too far. For the most part, there's no real link between which group a person was in and their family background, race, gender, education level, or income. In the Money Vigilance group though, the behavior hurt relationships rather than the bottom line. In another paper, Klontz and Klontz[12] surmised that money scripts are developed in childhood and often unconsciously passed down through generations of the same family. These scripts can be highly resistant to change, especially if they are associated with emotionally charged events. Klontz's four groups are mindsets, not skill sets. It seems that our emotional approach to money, when suboptimal, can hurt our finances.

Education alone will not fix money problems that these people encounter; often we must change our mindset. Once we make a middle-class income, more money does not fix problems because it's not the amount of money itself that is the problem, it is what the money represents to us.

To move up, we must face fears and examine some of the excuses that we use when we don't meet our financial goals. Sometimes those excuses are fully valid. For example, young people have had little time to accumulate wealth. In today's busy world, it's difficult for people with family obligations to work more or change spending patterns because that demands time, attention, and discipline—all of which are already scarce. For older individuals, habits die hardest, but they also die hard for some younger individuals as well. Klontz[13] estimated that only about 10% of us will maintain a healthier financial lifestyle two years after committing to change. He said, "that's a little depressing, but then, 1-in-10 people do change."

There are valid excuses for not improving today, but most of the valid excuses are temporary and can be overcome. There are also some excuses that may or may not be true. Some excuses, even if only partly true or are untrue altogether hurt us just because we let them get into our head and dominate our thinking when we face doubt or setbacks. Let's look at some of the common excuses, and why they're only sufficient to stop us if we let them.

"The system is rigged against me." This statement is true for us, and for everyone (but not always by the same amount). Another variation on this statement is, "the system is rigged against me because I'm a woman" (or, insert other demographic profile here). Again, there is some truth to this statement. Women live longer, so they arguably need to save more for retirement, yet statistically they are paid less. And, as family caretakers, they are more likely to have a break in their career which curbs their upward mobility and results of years of lesser or no income. That said, the system is generally not so rigged against a specific person that they cannot rise to the next economic level.

That is, most of our potential is bigger than our obstacles to moving forward. Nearly everyone who has succeeded has worked hard, and some do have to work harder than others. For those willing to work hard, who know what to do, and who can overcome the obstacles that are trying to hold them back, success is achievable, in spite of an unfair system.

"I am a victim of bad breaks." This excuse may be true to various degrees ranging from unquestionably true, to being untrue. We've all heard or known someone who suffered and survived an economic shock that would have taken most of us down. For some of us though, this excuse may be our view on the world whenever everyday life goes against our plan. Where there is a real problem, it must be addressed, and where possible, mitigated. For most of us though, our choices are that we can waste time on self-pity or we can work on solutions to our problems, but not both. When we take a step back, working on solutions is the better plan unless we just want attention and pity. This takes both mental and emotional discipline. It is easy to feel bad about ourselves but it is hard to take a step back to analyze and come up with a rational plan to solve the problem. One trick that we can use when feeling this way is to allow a set amount of time, but only a set amount of time, for self-pity. By budgeting an hour for self-pity, but only an hour, we could validate our feelings that bad things had legitimately happened to us, but the negativity does not consume our day, our creative energy, and our ability to enjoy the positive things in life. At first, the hour may not seem long enough, and it takes self-discipline to stick to that time table. Over time, an hour is too much, and finally, there just isn't enough room in our schedule to spend on that negativity. Self-pity may be justified, but it's expensive! Imagine how much we could save in an hour by cutting expenses (e.g. gathering coupons), investing in our education (as we do when we read a book), or working an extra hour on building a business that could bring us both income and more assets. And, often help is there if we reach out and ask for it.

"Money is not that important, and it may be evil." Money is important if the lack of money is causing us stress. That stress can cause us to be less

productive, both at work and with family, and interfere with our happiness. Some say that money is evil. In fact, a common misquote of the Bible says that "[m]oney is the root of all evil." The biblical passage actually says that the *love of money* is the root of all kinds of evil.[14] That is, money is not evil, but greed, or excessively prioritizing money, is.

"*I do not have enough time*." We have the same number of hours in a day as Beyoncé. We may have more demands on our time, but odds are good that it's been a while since we studied how we are spending our time. Even with very little time, we might be able to improve our financial situation slightly. In some cases, we can save time and advance financially. By reading this book, we are taking the first steps to using our time to improve our financial health. Keep on this path, and the rewards will accumulate.

"*I have too many obligations to take the necessary risks*." We think of successful entrepreneurs as risk takers. They are. We think of them as liking risk. They don't. They are just better at mitigating the risks that they can foresee. They have Plans B, C, and D ready in case plan A doesn't work out in their favor. They are constantly assessing and reassessing risks and expected rewards so that they can afford losses and profit from successes. We need to change the pattern of risk-taking from away from "taking as little risk as possible" to "taking measured, well-reasoned risks" where we too can profit from gains but afford the losses should they occur. Tying back to the earlier example where people prefer to gain $50 than risk gaining $100 or losing $50, entrepreneurs will ask if the loss is sustainable. They will consider whether they can achieve better than 50-50 odds. If they think that the loss is sustainable, and the odds are in their favor, they'll take the risk. And, who says we can't take the $100 and then quit before taking the next risk?

We take measured risks every day in the form of buying lottery tickets. I am not recommending playing the lottery. Ambrose Bierce has defined a lottery as "a tax on people who are bad at math," and as a financial strategy that's largely true, but what happens to people when they play and win a large amount very suddenly? Their problems go away, right?

Winning the Lottery

We play the lottery for different reasons, but most of the reasons have some dream of getting rich. While the odds of winning much in the lottery are very low, some of us believe that winning the lottery is our *best* shot at getting rich. But, what happens when our wealth catapults us across economic levels?

Often, in a matter of a few years, lottery winners are in worse financial shape than before they won the jackpot. On the surface, this seems strange because they've won enough money to last more than a lifetime. On the other hand, we all know people who can save a little something no matter how little they make, and we all know other people who will spend $1.10 for every $1 that they make. The worst thing for those who overspend may be to win the lottery, because they will overspend their winnings too; but unlike wages that are more easily replaced, the odds of winning the lottery again are extremely low so they ultimately end up in bankruptcy.

There's even a legendary lottery "curse." Past winners attribute thefts, divorces, murders, suicides, drug overdoses to having won the lottery. Sandra Hayes describes her emotional turmoil post-win, "I had to endure the greed and the need that people have, trying to get you to release your money to them....These are people who you've loved deep down, and they're turning into vampires trying to suck the life out of me." [15]

Richard Lustig, a seven-time grand prize lottery winner, is relatively happy and he thinks the curse is more about human behavior than the supernatural. He explains it this way, "[t]he reason why you hear those horror stories about people who win huge amounts like that and all of a sudden they're filing bankruptcy is because it's usually from people who have never had that kind of money before in their lives." He added, "[t]hey just go through it like crazy." [16]

That is, Lustig seems to concur that as people change economic levels, they need to change their skills, habits, and mindsets in order to maintain that new, higher economic level. Being a lottery winner will cause a sudden shift in wealth which will propel us through the economic ranks very quickly.

Gaining that much wealth so suddenly requires a change of behavior that many winners and their families are not able to pull off.

The rest of this book is a discussion about the necessary skills, habits, and mindsets in the individual economic levels, from lowest to highest, using a historical and sometimes world perspectives. Economic levels are culturally specific and do change over time. Importantly, there's a discussion of how to transcend from one level to the next higher level. After the highest economic level, there's a discussion about what to do when fortunes reverse. Reversals may be planned, as often happen when someone retires, but often reversals result from economic shocks like sudden unemployment or a severe medical illness in the family. Then there's a summary of the skills so that readers can use this book to track their progress without having to reread every chapter.

Notably, the title asks why everyone is not a millionaire, not a billionaire. And, in many expensive places, a million does not go very far. This leaves space for billionaires to step up and write books for millionaires to move up even further.

This book is based on years of professional and personal observation, experience in the financial industry, and having read and conducted academic work on how people spend money. However, not all rich people are the same. In fact, they're very different. Readers may not make it to millionaire status, but hopefully, most readers' finances will materially improve enough to more than offset the cost of this book. And, more money does tend to make life easier for most of us.

This book is different from other books on the market because while many books offer a lot of good advice, those books target readers in a specific economic class, teach them to succeed within that class, but then assume that they stay in that economic class where that advice continues to be both relevant and advisable. Indeed, some financial advice, like "live beneath your means," is fairly universal and true. However, most financial advice is not universal! Like medicine for a health condition:

- We can be prescribed the wrong advice for our financial condition.

- We can take good advice when there is better advice on the market, delaying our financial recovery.

- We can take the right advice for too long, which eats away at the effectiveness of the advice until it is nearly worthless, or worse, harmful.

So, the advice in this book is targeted according to specific economic levels. As we move up or down the economic ladder, we should change our skills, habits, and mindsets in response. We should also change the advice that we listen to. To understand which advice to take, we first have to understand our economic class.

Which Economic Class Are You?

The definitions of the different economic classes vary, so it's hard to categorize where we fit. However, salary range and median net worth are indicators that help economists, politicians, and money managers sort people by class.

Table 1: Economic Classes with Economic Indications[17]

Economic Class	Salary Range	Median Net Worth (based on 55 years old)
Lower-Lower	Less than $15,000	$1,250
Middle-Lower	$15,000–$24,999	$1,250
Upper-Lower	$25,000–$34,999	$34,375
Lower-Middle	$35,000–$49,999	$34,375
Middle-Middle	$50,000–$74,999	$168,500
Upper-Middle	$75,000–$99,999	$301,475
Lower-Upper	$100,000–$149,999	$644,100
Middle-Upper	$150,000–$999,999	$1,122,900
Upper-Upper	$1,000,000+	$1,122,900 +

For purposes of this book, the classes are broken down into lower, middle, and upper class, and then within each of these classes, there are three subclasses for a total of nine groups that will be covered in this book. And, class is as much a mindset or outlook as it is an economic concept.

Within the lower class, there's a lower-lower (lowest) class that resembles mere survival in extreme conditions. Then there's middle-lower class, which most of us would think of as the lowest class we would see in developed nations today. This class is impoverished and generally dependent on some type of government or other external assistance or is homeless. Then there's the upper-lower class filled with the working poor who generally make near minimum wage. While fully trying to participate in the workforce, this group has high economic insecurity and is in imminent risk of poverty when we encounter even a moderate economic shock like an illness that causes high medical bills or causes us to be unable to work for a short period of time. In some instances, this group represents entrepreneurs who are starting businesses with very little capital. This group has little to no savings, and very limited access to credit with reasonable terms.

Within the middle class, there's a lower-middle class that is sometimes called "the working class." This group is sometimes associated with semi-pro-fessionals and most craftsmen. There's some job security, but income for this household is just adequate. There's often some savings, but it may be in the form of pensions or home equity and can be undercut by a large economic shock. This group also includes undercapitalized businesses, which may have advanced beyond the start-up stage. The middle-middle class generally includes salaried workers with benefits at the lower end of a company's salary scale, including lower level managers for large companies. This is often where young, college educated professionals join the labor force. It also includes many of the best craftsmen and small business people who are modestly successful. The upper-middle class generally includes highly-educated, profes-sional, salaried workers, and middle management. It also includes successful small to mid-sized businesses. While wealth is used to measure millionaire status, income is one indicator of how fast we are likely to accumulate wealth. For the upper-middle class, yearly household income is probably approaching $100,000, U.S.

Within the lower-upper class, income tends to be more stable, but importantly, there's a net asset base that will cover most economic shocks. Assets are generally in the form of home equity, pensions, and perhaps long-term life insurance contracts. While the net assets are there, they may not be liquid enough to provide adequate access to cash flow without borrowing. The middle-upper class generally includes upper management, very successful entrepreneurs, celebrities, and some heirs. The upper-upper class, or "super-rich" can be thought of as the billionaire class. Yearly incomes commonly exceed $500,000 U.S.

The classes and subclasses are not separated by bright-line tests. We also must look at how our mindset towards money is evolving as we go up the economic ladder. We may be holding on to a "truthiness" that sounds good and works for others but is wrong for where we are now. And, regardless of what class we are in, nearly all of us are trying to get to the next one. Our family histories may be filled with generations going from very wealthy, learned professional classes to fleeing a country or losing everything in a war, to rebuilding and doing well again. Wealth is not permanent, and neither is poverty. This book will try to help us get a better foothold in climbing up to the next higher economic class from wherever we start.

We also must commit to change. Klontz found[18] that people are slow to change. After heart surgery, only about ten percent maintain healthier lifestyles two years after the surgery. People making financial changes fare no better, and are less likely to die, which should be a very strong incentive for change. We must be the one in ten that make and monitor the financial change process permanently.

That is easier said than done. In their book *Immunity to Change*,[19] Robert Kegan and Lisa Laskow Lahey teach people that have been resistant to reform how to overcome the large problems in their life. They argue that if we feel like there is a big problem that we've been unable to resolve, it is also because something that we have learned previously is interfering with the change that we are trying to make now. It's like driving with one foot on the gas and the other foot on the brake pedal. What you learned may not even be correct, or its application may be much more limited and therefore inappropriate in the current situation where it is interfering with the solution to our problem. In essence, earlier learning was appropriate for its time and circumstance, but that early learning creates an immunity to other learning that would contradict it—even when that other learning is appropriate to solve a big problem in our life.

In both their online Harvard course and their book, they outline a process that begins by our identifying a large goal that has been difficult for us to achieve and making a visible commitment to changing it. Unless we are strongly motivated to change, we generally won't, so this process may not work for minor changes. So, for example, if we want to prevent our children from having to support us in our old age, we might commit to increasing our net worth by saving now. From there, we would list what we are doing or not doing that may sabotage or slow the progress on achieving our goal. The obstacle to savings may be overspending in the present. But, these obstacles, they argue, are probably are not random. They actually help us achieve another, hidden goal.

For example, suppose we commit to increasing our net worth by saving 12% of our salary without increasing our debt, but we have a habit of spending money on the family beyond the basic food, shelter, and clothing. We also have a habit of spending more on clothes than we need. Using the Kegan-Lahey chart, our situation would look something like this:

Visible Commitment	Doing/Not Doing Instead	Hidden Competing Commitments	Big Assumptions
To provide for my family by increasing my net worth through saving 12% of my salary	Spend on family opportunities as they arise Purchase more clothes than I really need		

Now the self-reflection begins. Why would we do something that's contrary to a goal that's important to us? Previous generations have been judgmental and would have offered explanations like, "we're lazy," "we're undisciplined," "we spoil those kids too much," and "we're vain." Kegan-Lahey suggest that there may be a bigger, hidden goal that we *are* accomplishing instead of our explicit goal that we are not. For example, maybe we feel committed to ensuring that our family feels economically secure. This may be an important goal for us, especially if we were raised with the fear that there was never enough money, or that if there was enough money, there was just barely enough, and one economic setback could crush any economic security our family had. We may actually fear that by saying "no" to these small excesses, we are signaling to our current family that they, too, are on the brink of economic disaster. On the other hand, by spending more money than is needed on everyday items, we assume that we are accomplishing a very important, albeit hidden goal: we are signaling economic strength and ease which, we assume, will reduce our family's economic insecurity.

Visible Commitment	Doing/Not Doing Instead	Hidden Competing Commitments	Big Assumptions
To provide for my family by increasing my net worth through saving 12% of my salary	Spend on family opportunities as they arise Purchase more clothes than I really need	Make my family feel economically secure. (Extinguish the fear of economic peril.)	If I show my family that we can afford these extravagances, then I'm showing economic strength and they won't be economically fearful.

Our spending is not a by-product of being lazy or undisciplined. It is a by-product of caring for our family and not wanting them to know the fear that we have known. It's love. So, how do we meet both of our goals: making our family feel economically secure *and* save for the future? Kegan and Lahey suggest that we start by questioning our big assumptions and testing them in very safe, controlled, and small ways. For example, we might start by questioning whether there are other ways to show economic strength, like posting a chart showing progress toward a short-term goal like a family vacation. We might practice ways of saying "no" when asked for luxuries when our savings goal of 12% is not being met. We might say something like, "we can have this after we take care of a savings goal," or "we can have this next month if we still want it," or "we would love to get this for your upcoming birthday."

By working through financial issues with our fears in mind, we can reduce the resistance we have when we're trying to meet our most stubborn, important goals.

CHAPTER 2

Caveman Survival: Moving from the Lowest Level to a Middle-low Level

"District Twelve, where you can starve to death in safety."[20]

———————

Let's begin with a metaphorical illustration of how the financial rules change by class, why we don't change with them, and what happens if we do or do not change accordingly. Usually, the examples in this chapter aren't applicable to most of us in real life, because most of us have already ascended beyond this level.

Picture the poorest life possible. Like a caveman, we hunt and gather whatever food that we can find, and food of any kind is extremely scarce. Anything that is killed now may be the last of its kind and an end to future food altogether. Anything that is ripe now won't last very long before it rots. Every food is perishable, and there's no way to store food. Even if we could store food, how would we protect the stored food when we went out to look for more? We're literally living "hand-to-mouth" and probably thinking only for the short term. In this mode, survival is the goal, and that means, by and large, every man for his or herself.

Since the food sources are not varied, there is not a balanced diet, and since food takes so much energy to find, there's little energy left over to invest in and improve our lot. On the flip side, we really have little if any expenses. Where there is energy to invest in making life better, it's best focused on building tools for survival. These include anything that will help us find, kill and pick food, and anything to defend ourselves against predators.

From an economics perspective, life is lived at a financial break-even. We have no assets. We have no debts. No one would loan us something when we have no means of paying back the loan. We have no assets to take when we would default on paying back that loan, and our success at hunting means one more person is vying for food when there's nearly none to be had. Geographically, we do not travel very far from where we were born. Most travel is on foot, often over rough, and unfamiliar terrains.

Independence from others is key to survival so that no one takes our food from us when we're hungry. Consequently, we want the size of our family or social group to be as small as possible, except as limited by our own human compassion to nurture. We need strong hunter-gatherer skills to survive and thrive, and we must be . able to defend our kill from others who would try to take it from us. In economic terms, the main financial focus is to secure enough "income" in the form of food to live on (Marginal Revenue = Marginal Cost), for the very short-term, like "today." Our expected life span is not very long. In some cultures, we may actually be the food for other people, and we certainly are a food source for hungry animals. This is not a very fun life, so what is needed to transcend to the next economic level?

Our greatest need is a steady source of food, followed by shelter from the elements and outsiders, including animals and other people who want to take our food. Many of us are frequently "hangry." Because life expectancies are low, our parents probably won't live long, and because food is scarce, they won't want to provide for us longer than they must, and probably will be increasingly less able to do so. We must move from dependence to total independence as soon as possible, even if we are of an age where today we would still be considered a child. There are more moral dilemmas. We may kill other people to preserve our food source. We may steal. As explained in the Harlan Howard song "Busted" covered by Johnny Cash and Ray Charles, they explain that, "[w]ell, I am no thief, but a man can go wrong when he's busted."

Get Us Out of Here!

To be successful at survival, we must be skilled at getting food and eating it ourselves. Sharing outside of our immediate group is out of the question because food is so scarce. Sharing means that we go hungry and perhaps even starve to death because if we share the animal we just killed, and that animal is the last one, or we can't find another, we may starve. The exception is that we might get help from a closely-knit family. So, the key to survival at this dire economic level is selfishness.

But, to transcend to the next economic level, it makes sense to bargain for sharing food in some cases. That is, to survive, we must refuse to share; but to rise, we must learn to share wisely. These two skills, refusing to share and sharing wisely, are in direct contradiction to one another. It's that type of contradiction in skills that follows us as we try to rise up the entire economic ladder and sometimes trips us up if we refuse to adapt. What we learn at one level and what may be essential to survival can hurt us at higher levels, but naturally it scares us to abandon an important lesson that may have saved our life. So, we must understand what is needed, but we must overcome the fear to do what is needed. Understanding how rational fears turn into our own obstacles can be key to our own rising.

At the lowest economic level, humans who first learn to be wholly self-sufficient and then learn to share wisely will, on the whole, do better than those who learn to survive and refuse to share, but don't learn to share wisely as food becomes more available.

As food becomes more available, it makes sense to bargain with a few others who appear to be trustable. We strike deals along the lines of, "I will give you the leftovers from my kill, if you give me the leftovers from yours." Since food perishes quickly and cannot be stored or easily defended anyway, each of our marginal revenue (how many resources come into the household) increase at no marginal cost (no extra effort and without having to forego other resources), provided we and the people we bargain with honor the agreement (and don't also try to eat each other). In economic terms, Marginal Revenue still equals Marginal Cost, but the time horizon is lengthened to include multiple kills. The goal of this bargain is to eliminate draughts in our food supply. It works if we give away the excess that would rot for us anyway, and in the bargain, get excess food when we are unable to secure food on our own.

If We Know This, Why Don't We All Do This?

Some of us have learned the lesson of not sharing so well that we don't look for any other solution. Some remember sharing and the pain of going hungry, and we are too scared to try sharing in case we face the pain of going hungry again. Because sharing, even in the form of a sensible bargain, is so contrary to what we learned at the lowest level and some of us *fear* that sharing would make us worse off, no bargain is seriously contemplated or completed. Those fears may be justified at least in part, and especially when we are on that metaphorical bridge between economic levels. Progress up the economic ladder is usually in a two-steps-forward, one-step-back pattern, so it's not always clear what part of the economic ladder we're on. Making the sharing bargain only makes sense if there is enough future food for there to be excess food for us from time to time.

But, if there is enough future food to create a periodic excess sometimes and we do make that bargain, we are fed more often. And, if we are better fed, we may be better able to ward off illnesses and secure better shelter, increasing our chances of survival. We may also be able to use our alliance to increase our collective chances of getting more of a particular food. Two of us hunting together may be able to better corner an animal that would otherwise have gotten away. Contracting may also increase the diversity of our diet—you bring an opossum; I'll bring a salad. We then continue expanding our duo to a small tribe of vetted associates who help us secure what is possibly a year-round supply of food for everyone, with enough extra that some of us can stay home from the hunt and build shelters and tools. We huddle together in small groups, and by huddling, we are richer.

Being richer, a change of mindset and a change of habit is called for. We need to dispute our assumptions. Rather than assuming that all outsiders are bad, we must balance the risk that outsiders have not yet evolved to our way of thinking with the possibility that we might both be fed more often. But, we must do so cautiously—they may try to eat us! We may begin by safely leaving leftovers that would otherwise be wasted to those who we have observed to be good hunter-gatherers and appear not to be a serious threat to us. We begin to develop rudimentary negotiating skills.

We continue some old skills. We eat what we kill. We continue to defend ourselves. But, **we replace** isolationism with cautious observations of others and an openness to help others when we have excess resources. **We add** the concept of self-interested sharing in an attempt to build alliances. These changes fundamentally change the way we live our life. They bump us to the economic level where the goal is to survive to a level where we begin to build foundations for greater physical comfort and emotional growth. There may be no concept of money yet, only barter. We also begin building foundations for a diversified economy where a high tide lifts all boats. We adapt away from a solo existence to a huddled existence, adding a more complex social level than we otherwise would have encountered. Emotionally, we begin to learn how to trust and be trustworthy. That normally begins with family and by forming small communities based on mutual trust.

We haven't talked about huddling for love. So far, life is described as very selfish, without much regard to others. This is an over-generalization, but it has some basis in psychological theory. Abraham Maslow proposed a theory[21] derived from his study of the healthiest 1% of the student population. The resulting theory is often shown as a pyramid, with physiological needs that are common to everyone at the bottom, the need for safety that is common to most of us in the next highest level, etc. Self-actualization, a level that few of us reach, is the highest level. When a need is not met, a human might still survive, but at a minimum will feel anxious and tense. For most of us, the needs must be met in order. Each of the lower-level needs must be satisfied before the higher-level needs can be satisfied.

Figure: Maslow's Hierarchy of Needs, as shown in Wikipedia.org.

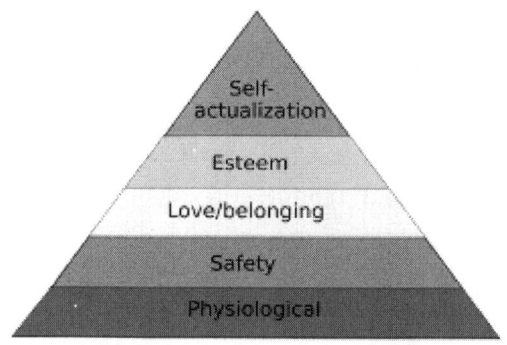

More explicitly, physiological needs are what we need to survive, including air, water, food, sleep and shelter. Sexual competition may be in this category in some cases. Safety needs include personal health and well-being and could be threatened by outside forces like war and natural disasters, or local forces like family violence. Economic safety is generally included here, and manifests itself in a need for job security, insurance purchases, and the tendency to save for a rainy day.

The next level is love and belonging, which includes developing deep and long-lasting relationships in families or social groups. The Esteem level acknowledges our need for respect for ourselves and from others. The top level of the pyramid is self-actualization, which is the need to realize our full potential.

While these levels appear separate in the pyramid, Maslow notes that the levels are not sharply divided, and are actually interrelated. The focus on certain pyramid levels may vary with our age. Later, Maslow expanded on self-actualization, believing that the only way to self-actualize is to become spiritual and contribute to a higher goal outside of oneself in the spirit of altruism.

Maslow's hierarchy applies to us, because while not written as a financial treatise, it does tell us how we prioritize our attention, including our financial attention. That is, while we may give money to charity (self-actualization and transcendence level), we will generally make sure that our family is fed first (our physiological needs are met). And, feeding and protecting ourselves and our family is central to this economic level and the next.

As such, we have a keen vigilance to threats at this level and a reduced sense of personal control than at other economic levels. As we ascend through the economic levels, the perceived threats are eased and perhaps because we are in a more insulated environment, our sense of personal control over the outcomes of our lives increase. But, for now, our now, the challenge is to survive, and especially to bring in enough food.

CHAPTER 3

From Ancient and Developing World Poverty to Most U.S. Poverty Levels: Moving from Middle-Lowest Level to the Top of the Lowest Level

"Well, I am no thief, but a man can go wrong when he's busted."[22]

This chapter is more applicable to the poor in developed countries, where we usually get some level of government assistance and may remain periodically hungry, but starvation—radical threats to health from malnutrition—is unusual. It applies to our homeless and intermittently homeless here. It also applies to those of us who normally have some type of day-to-day shelter from the elements, who are barely hanging on.

Once we are good at finding food (at least seasonally), we work on remaining safe from the elements and building alliances with others who can and will help us find more food, improve our shelter, and protect us against external threats like animals and other tribes. Our lifestyle has changed. We move from independence to interdependence on the group. We thrive by huddling together with others we can trust. Suppose food is sparse but not exhausted like in northern winters and suppose there's no good way to keep it from spoiling. It makes sense to have allies because we eat what we kill until we are full. Then we share the rest as part of a bargain. When others kill and we are hungry, we get their leftovers. Similarly, when we're joining with others in an economic support system, we do so for longer than a meal-to-meal basis. That is, we begin to plan for the near future, and the more economically successful that we become, generally, the greater the amount of time that we plan. For example, researchers found that New York taxicab drivers work until they earn their daily budget,[23] whereas MBA students reconcile their meals and entertainment budgets weekly and their clothing budgets monthly[24] and physicians reconcile their personal budget yearly.[25]

In developed worlds, we may be able to panhandle or access government or charitable assistance. Sometimes our neighborhoods band together for help and protection. In U.S. towns, there are often food stamps usable at grocery stores and charities operate food pantries in a way that prevents starvation, if not hunger. Some cities have homeless communities. Governments and charities might also help with housing. We may work part-time or full-time but irregularly. In some cases, it's possible to save, although generally only meager amounts. That doesn't stop our entrepreneurial spirit though. We may start small businesses that need very little money to found, often in an attempt to rise to the next economic level.

Big Words for Easy Ideas: What Is Entrepreneurship?

Entrepreneurship means starting and running an ongoing business. Essentially it means being self-employed. In a sense, at the lowest level, everyone was what we would think of as self-employed. As we begin to form groups, leaders and followers begin to emerge. This change parallels basic employer/employee relationships, where the leaders are closer to today's entrepreneurs and followers are closer to employees who largely do what they are told in return for a steadier source of food, shelter or other income. Where civilizations already exist, entrepreneurs seek out ways to provide for their families outside of, or in addition to being an employee. The rewards and risks of employees are different from those of entrepreneurs, so it makes sense to discuss the economics of being an employee and being an entrepreneur separately. The term "entrepreneurship" as it applies here assumes that the entrepreneur is intentionally involved in an ongoing business, as opposed to receiving a one-time or very limited time payment for a good or service. Normally, the entrepreneur, by definition, has begun to think further forward into the future than we did when we were in the lowest economic level.

Most businesses started at this level are service businesses that require little to no startup capital. These include housekeeping, daycare, and taking odd jobs. Where we sell products, we normally carry very little inventory and the per unit cost of that inventory is small. Still, many of our businesses are formed on a shoestring budget and economic corners are cut. For example, researchers in poor countries have found it hard to get poor farmers to purchase insurance, even when it pays them to do so.[26] This might be because immediate needs seem concrete, but the dangers of the future seem very abstract. We choose the concrete choice, even if it's wrong, exacerbating our poverty.

That does not mean that employees cannot save a million. Indeed, sometimes being an employee can be a less risky path, especially for those in higher earning jobs. But, less risk leads simultaneously to less potential loss *and* less potential rewards.

Life at This Level—Getting by Day to Day

Every economic level we are in colors our view of the world. Our places within the economic levels are more of a continuum, and our place in the continuum changes. We may move up and down through the continuum. The continuum itself also shifts as economies as a whole go through recessions and recoveries. But, our experiences change the way we see the world and how we behave in both small and profound ways: from where we shop, what we drive (if we drive at all), what kind of school we are likely to attend, and how successful we will be at that school, the kinds of jobs that we have access to, and the friends that we make. Economic class is a predictor of the degree of status, power, and perks that we enjoy daily.[27]

At this economic level, people may be "generationally poor" or "situationally poor." The distinction is important.[28] The generationally poor, defined as those coming from a family of two or more generations of poverty, have a different mindset than the situationally poor, and who were once middle class but are currently poor primarily due to adverse economic shocks. The situationally poor have a much better chance of rising out of poverty and are discussed in Chapter 11. Still, some of the circumstances associated with being poor pertain to both the generationally poor and the situationally poor. For instance, when our child is sick, and we must be at work, who takes care of the child?

So, what does income look like for people in this economic class? Household income sometimes exceeds our household needs, at least often enough to allow for a stable source of shelter. Most of us rent a home but are not homeless, and in the U.S. we have the basic health and comforts of indoor plumbing, some heating and maybe cooling, and a way to cook food and bathe. Houses are often crowded, and cluttered. Who can afford drawer organizers?

Our life expectancies are shorter than for those at higher economic levels. This might be due to additional stress. Women report feeling more stressed by finances than men, even after accounting for age, income, and taking care of minor children.[29] However, poorer mothers with minor children are the most financially stressed.

Lower life expectancies may also be due in part to the unaffordability of timely or preventative health care. Chronic exposure to threats, including physical threats of living in a more violent environment and financial threats of being one bad break away from homelessness, increases our stress levels, which is detrimental to our health over the long term.[30] And, we pay less attention to our health. For example, poorer people fail to take their medications more frequently than those in higher economic levels.[31] If bones break or injuries are sustained, or we lose teeth, we're more likely to learn to live with the problem than if we were in higher economic levels. And, fighting and physical violence are more common than at other economic levels.[32]

There's probably some attention within the family to the emotional needs of the family. Family also pulls together financially. Family and close friends are the best source of borrowing quick cash when we need them.

Our employment may be unsteady though, or may not be full-time. Our wages are generally paid based on the number of hours we work rather than as a salary. The hourly rate is generally low and may be the minimum wage allowed by law in our state. Even if paychecks are steady, our jobs generally come with little or no fringe benefits. There is no clear path to substantial economic advancement. Since it's "just a job," usually at minimum wage with little to no upward mobility, we quit frequently when working conditions are bad, but will work very hard if we like you.

Perceived threats are common: unemployment, eviction, inability to get needed medical care, legal advice, and financial help. Knowing someone who is in jail or on probation is common.[33] We band together for survival. We have greater compassion and prosocial behavior than those in the upper class, who in turn place a greater value on individuality and independence.

We have limited geographic access to jobs, because the jobs must be accessible with limited and often public transportation. So, these jobs tend to be in towns and cities where public transportation is available, or sufficient commerce is within walking distance. We can move if the income source or food source moves, but only if it doesn't move very far or very fast. And, separating from one's support group is more dangerous for us than for those in a higher economic class because of the lack of emergency funds to come back home if needed.

Where multiple low-paying job opportunities are available, we may not embrace the job as anything more than a paycheck. However, we may have the ability to diversify income sources. In small towns, we might be farming or doing "odd jobs" like occasional maintenance, cleaning or repair, or improvement of others' homes. Often, though, our own home remains unrepaired because we can't afford the cost for parts and tools to fix it. So, our households may have more than one income, especially if more than one adult resides in the home. Still, we report living paycheck to paycheck with expenses exceeding income, or with large debt and no emergency savings to insure against economic shocks.[34]

We also live with an income stream that is irregular. We don't know far in advance how many hours we will be scheduled to work, and with limited or unreliable transportation, that makes it hard for us to work more than one job. Our work schedule, and our pay, may be seasonal like working for public schools, or dependent on favorable weather conditions or a strong economy, such as construction work or roofing. Job loss is common, often for reasons outside of our control, and unexpected spikes in expenses are common as well making it extremely difficult to budget or save at this level.[35]

We commonly receive government and local assistance with housing, food, clothing, and medical expenses, especially if we have children in the household. Contrary to popular belief, little of that assistance comes in the form of welfare. The image of welfare to some is that we have a group of freeloaders who refuse to work and yet collect enough welfare money for necessities and a few luxuries that the working class desired but did not have. This impression comes in part from the design of the pre-Clinton welfare reform that, among other provisions, made welfare temporary. However, even when it was in its heyday, Kathryn Edin and Laura Lein interviewed hundreds of low-income single mothers across America and found that traditional welfare did not provide enough cash for the poor to pay their bills. Often, the welfare check was less than the mothers' rent. Most worked part-time, but "off the books." They stayed on the welfare rolls because they needed both the government assistance and the money from work to survive, given that job opportunities for this group paid the lowest possible legal wage, had few if any benefits, and was often irregular, seasonal, or part-time.

As of 2012, only about 1.4 percent of Americans received any cash assistance, and among the poor, only 10 percent get Temporary Assistance for Needy Families (TANF), which is the modern form of cash welfare.[36] TANF benefits are often limited to those making less than a third of the poverty line.[37] Those of us that collect this money generally feel stigmatized by society and want to get off welfare as soon as possible. Food stamps, now called the Supplemental Nutrition Assistance Program or SNAP, the Special Supplemental Nutrition Program for Women, Infants, and Children (WIC), and Medicaid are more common subsidies, and are available to both low-income working and non-working families.[38] Medicaid provides us with subsidized medical insurance, and if we have children, we can apply for Children's Health Insurance Program (CHIP) and perhaps state or local childcare vouchers. In some states, there is housing assistance. Housing subsidies may make public housing available (e.g. "the projects") or may come in the form of a housing choice voucher. The amount of this assistance and the amount needed to qualify, vary by state and costs of rents in various areas within the states. Most government assistance programs are certainly helpful but tend to assume that our income and expenses are predictable. They're not.

With most of us working at least part-time, we often qualify for a federal income tax credit called the Earned Income Credit (EIC) which provides or increases our tax refund every year when we file our taxes. About one in five Americans receive the EIC.[39] Combined with a common strategy of over-withholding federal income tax, this refund check is often the largest check that we receive each year. The expanded EIC is another feature of the Clinton welfare reform that, unlike welfare which is reduced when we work "on the books," actually rewards us for work. Under the Clinton welfare reform, the EIC was designed so that with one full-year, full-time, minimum-wage job, the EIC would pull a family of three out of poverty – almost to the dollar. [40] Since that time, the EIC combined with a minimum wage that has not kept pace with inflation, will no longer do that. But, there's not the stigma in our receiving EIC that there is when we receive welfare. However, EIC is only available to working families. If we have been laid off or had a sharp drop in income, we see a sharp drop in the EIC as well, just when we need it most. Because we're getting a refund, we don't mind paying about $200 per year in tax preparation fees, even though the preparation is free through community Volunteer Income Tax Assistance (VITA) programs. We'd rather pay a fee and be treated with dignity than to get a free service where we're looked down upon in some places.

The household groups in which we belong may expand some, but the expansion is net of some contraction in some areas. That is, our household size is starting to stabilize. Where we earn most of the income, we may begin to shift out of our group. For example, we may have little tolerance for those who refuse to work but want to share in the wealth that we earn. We start to distance ourselves from some of our poorer friends. Part of the reason for this is that we have changed, and we now have less in common with the people who are poorer and haven't. We begin to accumulate things and space for ourselves, and liking that extra comfort, we may begin to contract their social circle. Hence the saying, "not everyone that came with you can go with you."

When we earn our way out of this economic status we tend to make our social circle smaller still. Others interpret this as a lack of caring. At extreme levels it can be. The very rich have been shown to have less empathy than those of lower economic brackets. [41] However, there's also a healthy skepticism of unequal relationships, where we do most of the giving, and others show no signs of wanting to give back and keep the relationship balanced. That is, we take social measures to ensure that there is adequate income participation from everyone that can work in our economic circle. However, our social group tends to be growing more than it's shrinking, and the group now includes neighbors and work colleagues in addition to the family. There's also a role for churches and other values and interest-based groups.

Financial Life—Living Hand to Mouth

There is probably at least one wage earner in the household, but the pay may be part-time or inconsistent and at or near minimum wage. It is a daily challenge to maintain the constancy and sufficiency of that income and deliberately accumulate a cash cushion against economic shocks. Except for spending on children, and depending on the culture, the disabled, expenses should regularly be less than income for each individual. If we live near commercial centers or have online access, hunting for bargains becomes something of a sport, as does "extreme couponing," where we seek out coupons in papers, flyers, and online to drastically cut the cost of our purchases. However, our ability to absorb occasional bad events or "economic shocks" like missing a week of work due to illness remains low. And, that causes us a lot of anxiety which in turn hurts our health, making illness more likely.[42] Often, there's no affordable credit with which to pay for regular bills on top of these shocks, and no or little collateral to loan against or pawn. When these shocks occur, something must give. First, we juggle the bills, getting the terms extended. Often, we pay bills late. One source estimates that about one in six families pay at least one bill late in a year, usually resulting in late charges, and at least ten percent have had their phone or utilities cut off in the last year, resulting in costly reconnection fees.[43] If we can get credit, we feel that we must use it, even when the repayment terms are unfavorable.

Another source of funding is our friends and relatives, if they have the money and are willing to lend, but this works both ways: if we borrow, we've got to be ready to lend, which makes our cash outflows even less predictable. Many financial experts do not understand why we would lend money when we're often on the brink of bankruptcy.

They miss that:

1. we can't afford health or premium auto or income replacement insurance premiums for economic shocks.

2. The insurance probably wouldn't pay us after the deductible anyway.

3. We do desperately need some kind of insurance.

4. We informally insure each other with zero-interest loans when needed.

If we have an economic shock shortly after we loan our money out, we could become insolvent. But, this system is often less risky and less costly than keeping our money ourselves but not having anyone to borrow from if we really need it. We have learned a lesson about contracting that we needed to learn at the lower level and we are stronger for it. Still, borrowing from friends and relatives also can cause tension in our relationships that remains at least until the money is repaid.

Mostly though, we need to have a steady, reliable source of income in addition to socially contracting to protect against shocks. In economic terms, marginal income equals or begins to exceed marginal cost on a longer, consistent basis.

What Is Needed to Transcend?

When marginal income does exceed marginal cost, we start to profit as a household, and there is an opportunity to save or buy assets that build family wealth. This does not necessarily mean that we have a savings account. It may mean that we buy a freezer to store and/or protect food or, where we are an entrepreneur, invest in better business tools. In the short run, the concept of **net income** is new, whereas before we were lucky to breakeven. However, we don't yet have net income *stability* or significant asset accumulation, so net income is likely temporary. And, net income only occurs if we develop a new skill—restraint from spending and consuming all of today's income.

When we can spend, we are tempted to spend too much or spend on the wrong things. This seems to make sense to those of us moving up from a lower level because we could never preserve our food and protect our windfalls, so better to relish in them now until they are exhausted. But, at this level, we can preserve and accumulate wealth. We don't always do so, though. Instead of saving for economic shocks, some of us succumb to impulse buying, which can be defined as buying goods and services because of a sudden whim rather than as an execution of a financial plan.

Five reasons we overspend are:

1. We love shopping or "retail therapy," which sometimes feels empowering.

2. We want to avoid feeling bad in the future, thinking that we've missed out on a deal.

3. We use somewhat convoluted rules of thumb—that marketers have figured out and have learned how to capitalize upon—that make our desired purchase seem like a good value. This is "the more you spend, the more you save" argument.

4. We think this purchase will change our life—we'll exercise more, or cook healthier meals, etc.

5. We do want to save, and the discounts on the purchase are so attractive that buying makes sense.[44]

Of these five reasons, only the last one actually helps us financially. The other four reasons can actually hold us back from becoming richer by wasting money on things that don't earn a return or protect us from economic shocks.

Living beneath our means at this level generally means our stress is reduced by more than the stress of the temptation to overspend. If we increase our lifestyle, the financial stress increases also, undoing one of the benefits of our making more money. Without extra income, there never was much of a chance to save and accumulate assets. Now, we may accumulate some assets. These assets may symbolize status to our friends. But, if we pay careful individual attention to asset accumulation, we can use these assets to move up to the next economic level. But, some of our friends might get jealous. That makes our assets a target for theft and consequential risk to family. The emotional manipulations of people who we've loved so dearly begin, and they can cut deep. That is, spending or sharing income at this level may seem wiser in the short-term than accumulating assets, because anything that is saved would just be stolen anyway, or someone we love may try to guilt us out of it. Consequently, net income tends to be spent as incurred.

In this economic level, we routinely receive free assistance from the government or local charities, at least occasionally. Sometimes the assistance is overt, but sometimes it is more hidden like receiving an earned income credit when filing federal income taxes. This assistance can be invaluable, especially as it pertains to basic needs like housing stipends and grocery stipends. Rarely is this assistance enough to get by, though. So, we commonly make a little money on the side or work off the books to make ends meet. We fish, hunt, or prepare a garden for food. We take on odd jobs, often for cash. We also shop at second hand or thrift stores for necessary goods to keep our expenses as low as possible.

But What is Needed to Transcend to the Next Level?

Some start small businesses to move up, but most promises of fast cash are more trouble than what they're worth and benefit the people we buy them from. For small businesses and employees alike, at this economic level, a few general rules, regularly practiced, may work best.[45] The most basic rules for us are:

1. Keep business cash separate from household cash.

2. Keep business bank accounts separate from household bank accounts.

3. Keep accounting records of what comes in and what goes out.

4. Plan for what is likely to come in, and what is likely to go out; budget.

5. Learn how to formally calculate income and cost of goods sold.

One place to start is for us to separate business and household "accounts," even if those accounts are informal rather than official bank accounts. That way, there should be enough money to keep our business running. One low income but industrious entrepreneur worked only in cash. She was not financially schooled, but she still divided her money into household and business accounts. Her two "accounts" were the right cup and left cup of her bra.[46]

The next step for us is to study where the household income and expenses normally come from. That's one reason why budgeting is so important. That's true for us when we're employees as well. Most of us don't even know what's in our paycheck and what has come out of our paycheck.[47] Often, we are so focused on other things that the everyday spending gets away from us. Once the regular patterns are identified, we can change them if they are not in line with our big picture goals.

Next, we need to plan for irregular expenses (economic shocks), like unexpected medical expenses. Most of us do okay with regular expenses, but economic shocks are hard on everyone, especially us, because we simply have less cushion to absorb a large, sudden, fixed expense. Our brains themselves may be hardwired against saving.[48] Experience at the survival level left us unprepared to save, or even warned us against saving. And, if we must come up with this cash suddenly, we often go to people who would prey on our vulnerability with things like payday or car loans with very high interest rates that we can't reasonably pay off.

It's helpful to allocate our income into expense categories that Richard Thaler[49] (1999) calls mental "buckets." Having a few (different sized) buckets mean that we could run out of pizza money, indicating that it was time to eat in from groceries we've already bought, but have enough money to cover the cost of a home air conditioner, which of course costs more than a pizza. The pizza bucket is used up; the air conditioner money is not.

We also need to have some cash at home to save for economic shocks. We need to set savings goals with some of money set aside just for business and household emergencies. The goals may be a dollar amount or a percent of income. Even when we fall short of our savings goals, we statistically save more than if we had never set the goals to begin with.[50]

Once our goals are set, the next decision is where to save. Common wisdom says to save in bank savings accounts, but many of us are suspicious of banks in part because the interest rates on savings can be very low and bank fees can be very high. Banks are there to make a profit; these concerns are reasonable. Being a small customer in a large international bank is to be very insignificant indeed. In most towns though, there is a local credit union. These credit unions are often not-for-profits, which means that they are set up to serve customers many of whom have low bank balances like us. The money in individual accounts is insured up to $250,000. The interest rate on credit union savings accounts is usually competitive. Even if the credit union name is something like "Army Navy Credit Union," these credit unions will often take any of us living in that same geographic area, even if we have never been in the army or navy, and never had credit or been a credit union member before. Still, while credit unions are a great place to start a savings account, it's wise to cross-shop all the credit unions and banks in the area to find the highest interest rate and the best fit.

We'll be tempted to spend or stop saving. When that happens, it's sometimes helpful to remember where not planning led to something disastrous. That memory can help us overcome hard wiring against saving *now*. The easiest way to save is usually to put aside money automatically. In some lucky cases, we can do this through a payroll deduction at work. Otherwise, we can make regular visits to the credit union. By putting money away where it's still safe and accessible but a little harder and less convenient to reach, it's more immune to overspending on short-term things that may be fun, but undo progress toward our long-term goals.

For many of us, we get a chance to save at tax time if we qualify for the Earned Income Credit (EIC). The EIC is designed to give those of us who are lower income and continuing to work a tax refund. About one in five receive the earned income credit, a tax credit for working families. [51] Of those of us receiving that refund, nearly four in ten of us initially save it. Because this refund is large for us and received once a year, we anticipate it, and plan to save at least some of it to get ahead. And although we may treat ourselves to a little something, we generally try not to use it for everyday expenses. Where we do use this money for everyday expenses, it may be because we got behind in the heating bill knowing it's illegal for the utility company to cut us off when it's still cold, for example,. We knew we should receive our EIC check before the weather warms. The once a year EIC feature allows this money to accumulate nearly effortlessly without our having to exercise constant self-control over the course of the entire year. It reinforces our determination to save and thus better our financial lives. Halpern-Meekin et al. (2015) estimate that 17% of the EIC is initially saved, while 21% is devoted to expenditures that help us get ahead like education, home repairs, purchasing or repairing a car, buying a durable good like a freezer that will help us save money over the coming years. [52] We usually do tap part of the initial savings over the next six months, but we draw this money down to increase our upward mobility or substantially pay off debt, which we do not do and maybe cannot do with our ordinary incomes.

Once we know how much there is to spend after budgeting something for shocks, our next step is to learn to save on regular expenses, like buying in bulk when the items bought are on sale and will be used before they spoil or otherwise become worthless. Little changes here can have a big percentage impact especially when these items are used regularly, like not overusing laundry detergent or toothpaste. For example, laundry detergent caps are often used to measure the amount of soap in a load. We know that measuring is important so that we don't flood the laundry with soap suds exploding out of the washer. But, while the cap on the detergent can be used to measure, we're generally not supposed to use a capful. The cap on one Gain laundry detergent has 5 markings, and room for two more. For a medium load, we're supposed to fill the detergent to between marking 2 and 3. When we fill the cap, we're using over two times the amount we're supposed to use, and we wash often, and detergent is expensive. Learning even one household tip like that one helps us cut the laundry detergent expense in half. We look at fuel economy tips, like tire inflation, for cars, etc. Each over-use wastes little, but over a month, a year, or a lifetime, we can greatly overspend without realizing it.

That's another key: we need to begin to think over a longer-term horizon. We anticipate savings needs for the next week, month, and year. As we move up the economic ladder, the time horizon over which we budget should continue to lengthen, and for most of us it does. [53] And, it is very helpful if we have a mentor to get to the next level because the social rules change, and the mentor can help guide us through.

We must believe that we deserve to move up. That belief may not be necessary to make money, but it is necessary to keep the money we make. Recall that the Brad Klontz believes that there may actually be a psychological condition called "money avoidance," which in extreme cases even presents as self-sabotaging one's own financial condition.[54] Corroborating his point, Winkelmann, et al. (2010)[55] found that it takes about two years before lottery winners feel that they 'deserve' their good fortune. Think about that. Lottery, which is pure luck and zero skill, is open to anyone of any character. Yet, when we win, we don't believe we are entitled to an even shot at pure luck.

All of these changes represent a change to habits or thinking. But, do we add these changes to our existing toolkit, or replace some old habits with new ones? Even if we want to change, habits are hard to break. They're automatic, and we may not know what to replace them with.

If We Know What Is Needed Why Don't We Do This?

Because it is contrary to what we learned and believe worked at the lower levels *and* if we were to have done this when we were poorer, we fear we would have been worse off. Those fears may be justified, at least in part. These fears leave us hesitant, like driving down the road with one foot on the gas and one on the break. As discussed earlier, we need to identify them, safely test them, and adjust them based on the results of our testing.

For example, saving is to some extent betraying our lower income culture. Richard Sennett interviewed 150 first-generation Euro-American immigrants and found that when families chose to leave the old neighborhood to begin life in the suburbs, feelings of guilt and isolation continued throughout their life. On the other hand, those that stayed behind felt trapped.[56]

Any extra money we have is shared and we expect others to share with us should we need their extra money. What's not shared is spent on entertainment which reduces the stress of everyday life. Ruby Payne explains, "[t]here are always emergencies and needs; one might as well enjoy the moment."[57] Moving up brings contempt from our friends and family, who question whether we now think that we're too good for them. It is common to repeatedly give money to a relative who will not work, even if it means one's own household bills go unpaid. We may loan a car to a relative who does not have insurance and allow them to move in with us.

Another reason that we don't move up is that we are just so busy with other things and getting out of poverty requires a plan.[58] We can be out of energy and out of time. When this happens, we actually don't have the mental energy, called "bandwidth,"[59] to process every decision in life, and our actual IQ falls. Each one of us, as our economic circumstances fall, tend to get dumber, and each one of us tends to get smarter, as measured by IQ, as our economic circumstances rise. That is, we're not poor because we're dumb. We're dumb because we're poor.

Being unable to cope with the cognitive load of all the decisions that need to be made every day, use rules of thumb called "heuristics," to make decisions. To move up though, we need to recognize the heuristics that we use, question them one at a time, and change the ones that don't fit. We need to become very aware of our everyday life, not just at the point we are making a purchase. And, we need to start by asking if each heuristic is in our best interest in the longer run.

Getting out of poverty also requires *constant* resistance to temptation. That's difficult because self-control is a depletable resource that wears away as we get tired.[60] Some of us have difficulty with self-discipline. This can start at an early age and be a powerful predictor of success. One psychologist, Walter Mischel, studied the ability of individual children ages 3–6 to delay gratification, then followed their success in later years.[61] The experiment involved children getting a treat of their choice like a marshmallow which the children could eat immediately. However, if they could wait for 15 minutes without eating the treat, they'd get a second treat. One-third of the children who attempted patience were able to wait the full 15 minutes, earning the extra treat. In follow-up studies, children who could delay gratification tended to have higher SAT scores, levels of education, and lower body mass index. Thus, the "marshmallow test" is considered to be one predictor of later life success among young children. For poor adults, the cost to succumbing to temptation is high, and it is regressive, which means that those of us who have less wealth pay a higher cost as a percent of our total consumption than we would if we had more money.[62] Dan Bjorkegren found that for the poorest group of people in his study, the "temptation tax" was as high as 10% of their total consumption, but fell to as low as 1% in the group of people who were wealthier.[63]

Some of us make up our mind to save *tomorrow,* and that tomorrow gets delayed indefinitely. Called "present bias" by psychologists and "hyperbolic discounting" by economists, the result is the same: about half of us would rather have $100 today than be rewarded with $120 in a year, even though that extra $20 represents an extra 20% for doing nothing more than being patient.[64] As valuable as that extra $20 is, it's worth waiting for, provided we can afford to wait while still providing for our basic needs without incurring costly late fees like reconnection fees for utilities and interest on payday loans that eat up more than the $20 savings bonus.

At this level, we may still be fearful if we delay gratification in favor of saving. At this economic level, we may be afraid that if we don't enjoy excess money now, it won't be available later. It might be stolen, or lost, or clawed back by a bank in bank fees. It might be used for other things that aren't fun. It might reduce our government assistance. We might feel that our savings may be too small to make a difference but spending now makes a positive difference. We might find out that we can't meet our savings goals, which would mean that we and our family are trapped in poverty forever. At least now, there is hope. To save, we will be asked to give up the few pleasures that we have in life, like smoking. These fears can haunt us.

To move up, we must identify what fears we have, and challenge those assumptions. This can be done as we start saving for something small but important on a regular basis. Saving is a new skill, because at lower economic levels, there's nothing left over to save, and no way to preserve and protect what we want saved. At this economic level though, maybe we save a little, for emergencies. By labeling what we are saving for, we are less likely to spend the money on other things. We identify ways that we can save a little, perhaps by cutting costs. By regularly saving, we also make savings a habit. We may not be using a bank yet, but we can add to our savings tools as our savings grow.

However, we also must build slack into a budget. Unforeseen rising prices will use up some of that slack, but another reason for slack is that budgets that are too restrictive tend to frustrate us, and then we give up on the budget altogether when we take a few small luxuries for ourselves. Where possible, we should be on the lookout for free luxuries, like watching a sunset or using many of the parks and recreation programs offered by towns and cities. Still, just the freedom to spend a little bit of money on a small luxury is a psychological reward for being disciplined with the rest of the budget and reinforces to us that budgeting is working. So, savings on costs is split between fun and our short-term savings goal for economic shock. Once we know we can save a bit, saving through withholding from our paycheck for retirement if our employer offers that option,[65] even though it may be very far off, is an outstanding goal.

Actually, the further off retirement is, the easier it may be to save for, because the amount of weekly withholdings can be much smaller due to the return on investment being compounded over a longer period of time.

What Is Compound Interest, and How Does It Work?

Interest expense on car, home, and credit card loans can be figured two ways: as simple interest or as compound interest, which is better for the lender. Nearly every loan agreement uses compound, not simple interest. But, let's look at simple interest first. At a 10% simple interest rate, borrowing a $100 would mean paying $10/interest every year. So, at the end of 4 years, we'd owe the original $100 + (4*$10) = $140. With compound interest, we'd owe more. In the first year, we would still owe $10 of interest. In the second year, we would owe 10% on the $100 borrowed plus the $10 of last year's interest. We'd owe $11 in interest for that year, and each year the amount of interest continues to rise.

When we invest in a savings account, interest is normally compounded. But, we are receiving interest income. So, the same compounding that works against us when we borrow, works for us when we invest. And when interest rates are constant, the advantage we receive grows bigger with each successive year that the money is invested. Most of us understand that saving early for retirement is better than starting the year before retirement, but most of us don't have a clue how big a difference starting early can make.

Let's take an example. Suppose we want to save $1 million for retirement, and historically our investments return 7% per year, compounded monthly. To reach our goal, we'd need to save $263.71/month if we started in our twenties, which is about 45 years out from retirement. That's stiff, but it may be doable, especially if we start saving as soon as we enter the workforce and use tools like payroll deductions so that this money is taken out first, before our brain registers that we have the money and we are tempted to spend it on extra clothes, eating out, etc. Now suppose instead that everything was the same except that we started saving 10 years out from retirement. That should be enough time, right? After all, the early years are focused on building a career and family, and the early years of a career often come with low pay. In those last ten years, we would need to save $5,777.64 per month, and that may be more than we actually earn. Frustrated, we may save nothing, and never be able to retire. Of course, another plan exists where we don't need a million dollars: start immediately, but start with low monthly payments, say $50/month. Over 45 years, that alone will grow to over $189,000.

It may be possible to add a bit more, say, $5 per month every year, which would increase the retirement fund as well. That, though, takes a lot of discipline, especially in years where there are no raises. Still, as we rise through the economic levels, we are able to take more control of our lives, including our financial lives.

Even If We Could Save That Much, Where Would We Put It?

Most of us savers at this level have an informal account, adding a checking account followed by a savings account, followed by a retirement account.[66] If we know that we are prone be tempted to spend what we would really rather save, we hide our money. One person is known to have frozen her credit card in a block of ice. She had access to it if she needed it, but it was inconvenient to spend on impulse buying. Sometimes entrust the money to a close friend or family member, so it will be harder to spend. Of course, that only works when those close to us have more self-control than we do.

Retirement savings are set up to be harder to access and this is a good choice because in the U.S., Social Security alone will not be enough for us to retire. Normally, an employer-sponsored retirement plan is a good and easy way to save because even if we become unemployed, anything that we contributed plus what it earned or lost is owned by us and can be moved if we change employers. However, U.S. employers make no retirement contributions or have structured plans for two-thirds of us. That leaves us on our own. The U.S. government knows this and if we earned money during the year, the government will match part of our retirement savings contributions through tax credits. The most applicable tax credit is the Retirement Savings Contributions Credit or "Savers Credit."[67] Taxpayers who are 18 years or older and are not full-time students or dependent on another's return can use up to 50% of the first $2,000 of retirement funds invested as a tax credit, which works to reduce our taxes due. We get this credit *in addition to* applicable tax deductions (or exclusion from income if the plan is administered by an employer). Over 65% of taxpayers qualify for this credit, so why don't more of us save for our own retirement? One researcher asked this question and found that while about 14% were happy with their retirement savings and 12% thought that they were too poor to save anything, about 13% failed to set up their retirement because it wasn't convenient to do so.[68] The government has responded by encouraging employers and employees to set up Individual Retirement Accounts (IRAs) and other pension funds. They also developed a useful, thoughtful tool to help those in the lowest economic levels save small amounts, in "MyRA" (pronounced My-ra) accounts.[69] However, just two years after its launch, it was discontinued largely for political reasons.

We Can Also Build a Skill Set to Be Better Shoppers and Reduce Our Necessary Living Expenses

Wealthier people think we are bad with money. In truth, we are excellent at keeping expenses low. Many know which churches and sections of town have the best rummage sales. We know when stores throw out their expired medicines. We know which pawn shops sell cheap DVDs. We know how to live without electricity and a phone. We know which churches provide emergency food and shelter. We know how to get and use food stamps and where the free medical clinics are.

To further reduce our expenses, we need to hone our math skills so that we better understand the costs of what we buy and how those costs are marketed—or worse, hidden. For example, we can become better shoppers if we know the difference between 50% off and buy one and the second item is 50% off. In the first case, each item that normally costs $10 now costs (50% x $10 =) $5, so 2 items would cost (2 x $5 =) $10. It's mathematically the same as buy-one-get-one-free. That's a much better deal than in the second case, buy one and the second item is 50% off. In that case, the first item still costs $10, but the second one (only) costs (50% x $10 =) $5. So, in the second case, the entire purchase price is ($10 + $5=) $15. This is substantially more than what the same two items in the first case cost, but the language is confusingly similar. On purpose. Marketers word things this way so that we will pay more while still thinking that we got an outstanding, 50% off deal. However, it's mathematically the same as getting (only) 25% off each item. And, 25% off wrapping paper at a higher-priced store can still be more than full price at a dollar store.

Marketers spend a great deal of time and money watching our purchasing patterns. Normally, we are way too busy to think through every single decision thoroughly, so we use rules of thumb. For example, packaged grocery items are sold in different sizes. In decades past, the largest size was the best value for the money, as measured by dollar cost per ounce. This was because there was much less packaging for one large item than for two smaller items. Less packaging meant less cost, and that lesser cost was at least in part passed down to consumers. We consumers got in the habit of buying the larger sizes whenever we could afford to buy that product as a thrifty way of saving money, provided that we would use the greater amount of the product before it spoiled. It was a win-win. We bought more from the seller, and we saved money in the long run by doing this. Marketers caught on that we were habitually buying in bulk where we could. So, some of them changed the pricing structure so that the larger size now cost *more on a per unit basis* than the medium size. This is what is happening in the pictures below.

Example of Unit Pricing: Two Sizes of the Same Brand of Rice and Their Pricing

On the same day, same time at local grocery store, we were given a choice between two 14-ounce boxes of the same brand of rice (28 ounces in total), for $4.00; or one 28-ounce box of rice for $4.21. And, we didn't have to buy both boxes of the medium size to get a good price. We could buy just one box for ($4.00/2=) $2.00 if we want. In this case, it not only costs more in total for the bigger box of rice, it costs more per ounce. The medium size is the better value, by about 5%. That's $.20 here, but it's five dollars a week for $20 a month or $240 a year if we spend $100 a week on groceries. Put another way, we eat two weeks out of the year for free. To avoid doing math on everything we buy, we can refer to the unit price, which is where the seller has done the math for us. In this case, the unit price is 14.29 cents on the medium box and 15.04 cents on the larger box. We don't have to think deeply, we just have to know to compare prices on a unit price basis.

Marketers also assume that we consumers will jump at tax free weekends. In many states, there is a week or so where no sales tax is assessed on clothing, school supplies, and other things that people might need to further their education.[70] They often compete with sales prices of 10%–15% in addition to the savings we realize by not paying sales tax. That sales tax rate itself can be high. For example, in Texas, the sales tax rate is 8.25% in some cities. So, together with 15% off from the seller, we can save about 23.5%. That sounds great! But remember, that's after marketers have figured out that we don't like taxes, and how to profit from our tastes. Had we gone shopping the week before, many of those same stores had 25% off, which is a bigger savings than during the sales tax holiday. So, what the state intended to give to us (8.25%), some stores effectively took back by reducing the discount that they were offering for that sales tax holiday week only.

As poorer people, we look for and often catch these tricks. We are actually better and smarter about making ends meet *now* than our wealthier friends. We respond more rationally to economic stimuli. For example, when excise taxes on cigarettes go up, both the poor and the wealthy smokers respond by buying less. When the sales tax is hidden though, we catch this and respond; the wealthy tend not to.[71]

We are more vigilant about what we spend total and what each individual item costs then our wealthier friends.[72] However, the laser-like focus on today brings some negative consequences of ignoring the planning of our welfare for tomorrow.[73] But, we are "anything but myopic. Instead, it is the context of scarcity that makes us all act that way."[74] We are still limited by circumstances beyond our control.

Poverty *itself* taxes the mind, in part by reducing our fluid intelligence and executive control.[75] We are all faced with choices, but when there is low income, there is not much slack to cover an error. So, with relatively more at stake, making choices is harder. And, generally, it is not enough to just work harder. We are more prone to errors and less able to absorb them than if we were in a higher economic level, which increases our stress and our likelihood of failure.

Yet, to the extent that we succeed, we not only increase our wealth, we increase our health and our IQ and we reduce our stress level. And, progress, even though it generally comes unevenly, in a two-steps-forward, one-step-back kind of way, can give us hope and a sense of achievement, especially as it also benefits our children. And, it's important.

One young mother never held a steady job but determined that she was better off on government assistance than having a paying job where she in turn had to cover childcare costs and the cost of her family's medical insurance. One day, her son was in a mild fight with a school bully. No one was hurt, but her son was accused of assault by the bully's family, which resulted in suspension and criminal charges. With no money for a private attorney, a public defender was assigned. Overloaded and underpaid, the public defender convinced the family to take a deal resulting in probation rather than asserting self-defense. This is somewhat understandable from an attorney's point of view and an overworked court's point of view, but the result may have been very different if the family could have afforded a private attorney. And, in addition to court and costs for transportation to probation, there are psychological costs just from being incarcerated, however briefly.

The poor are disproportionately represented in the U.S. prison system. And, merely being incarcerated may prompt the prisoner to act more like a criminal, even when the prisoner is completely innocent. In the landmark Stanford Prison Experiment, innocent college students were randomly assigned to play the role of "prisoner" or "guard." Those assigned the role of prisoner were arrested by the Palo Alto police department, deloused, dressed in prison garb, chained and transported to the basement of a Stanford University building that had been converted into a jail. Both prisoners and guards began to internalize—not just act out—their given, random roles. A prison riot broke out. One prisoner developed a physical rash when his "parole" was denied. In just 6 days, the experiment was terminated for fear of the harm to the participants.

How Can We Help?

As family members, we must weigh in on how much to help, which is expected in a communal culture, and how much to have people "stand on their own two feet." We can also give advice, not just our money. As any advice to any audience, the advice we give should be tailored to that audience. It is probably more likely to be taken if given in small, frequent doses with reminders, since life is overwhelming. For example, studies show that savings increased by 6% by sending a monthly reminder to save by either text or letter.[76]

Societally, this is the subject of ongoing political and social debate. Stepping off assistance can be very expensive, especially when a household has small children that must be cared for as in the instance of a sole parent reentering the workforce. The lack of assistance can be devastating for these families, expanding the circle of poverty. Tens of thousands died from starvation and from diseases related to malnutrition (like the vitamin deficiency disease, pallegra), during the great depression of the 1930s,. Children are particularly vulnerable because their bodies and minds are still developing and arguably poverty is not their fault.

Shafir and Mullainathan, authors of *Scarcity, Why Having Too Little Means So Much*[77] suggest that a slow weaning off assistance, like a one-for-two reduction or phaseout of assistance may be best, as people earn more. Derek Thompson[78] recommends that U.S. policy makers should change the rules to be more consumer friendly to those just beginning to save or get credit. The Obama administration had responded by developing government sponsored MYRA accounts, but these were quickly rescinded by the Trump administration.

In many ways, we may have governmental or other assistance, but that keeps us alive. Moving out of an American standard of poverty is mostly on us. The next rung on the socioeconomic ladder is also uncomfortable, but provides more stability, comfort, and hope than where we are now, so most of us try.

CHAPTER 4

We Are the Best Bargain Hunters, When We Have Money to Spend— Moving Out of the Upper-Lowest Level and Making It to the Lower-Middle Class

"I was not from a middle-class family at all. I did not have middle-class possessions and what have you. But I had middle-class parents who gave me what was needed to survive in society."[79]

The people of this chapter are common in the U.S., and our number is growing as the income divide has widened over historically normal levels.[80] What does life look like for us here, broadly and financially?

Life at This Level—We Get by With a Little Help from Our Friends

Our life is better than at lower socioeconomic levels, but we don't have it made yet and we still need our friends. We still feel limited by lack of resources and opportunities. It seems that uncontrollable social forces and the power of others still have a strong grip on our lifestyle.[81] Success depends largely on how well we can read other people and are able to rely on and help out others.[82] We see the key to our success as being based on maintaining relatively communal strategies. In turn, that may make us more attuned to our partner's emotions[83] and be more supportive of our social group than concerned with the equality of our relationships.[84] Fitting in and maintaining relationships is more important than standing out in a crowd.[85] This makes us more empathetic than our wealthier friends.[86] Independence is only beginning to take root.

We begin to have paper or electronic documents for life milestones such as: birth certificates, driver's licenses, immunization records, rental agreements, paycheck stubs, bills, and high school graduation transcripts. We increasingly use an online checking account and bill pay. We might have and use a credit card or a savings account. Our IQ is rising with our income.[87] We know at least vaguely what an annuity is. We understand the basics of term life insurance, and might have that, as well as health insurance, possibly disability insurance, and long-term care insurance. We also insure our home and auto.

There is probably at least one wage earner in the household with a fairly steady job, but the pay may be near minimum wage. It is still a challenge to deliberately accumulate a cash cushion against economic shocks. We are more likely to have intermittent use of independent transportation, like being able to Uber. Still, we tend to travel only for work and not very much for leisure. If we do travel for leisure, it's likely to be low cost, like camping, or staying with friends or relatives. There are probably dreams of saving for assets that reduce lifetime expenses: saving for buying a house rather than renting or saving for an education that produces higher lifetime earnings. Life is still communal.

Other friends or family members may live with us, and we network with other people, helping each other regularly. But, we might have a bit of personal space like our own room, and the number and composition of our household is more stable than when we were poorer. We try to help each other up, rather than shut each other out. We encounter fewer fatal threats than our poorer friends and have a greater locus of control over our life. However, we run a very real risk of dying from drugs, poisoning, or suicide.[88]

Financial life is still especially stressful.[89] The top financial concerns are: not saving for retirement, having no emergency fund,[90] living beyond our means, and having a relatively large amount of debt. We live paycheck to paycheck. In 2015, 63% of *all* Americans said that they had no emergency fund for a $1,000 emergency room visit or a $500 car repair.[91] And the situation is not improving. In 2011, almost half of Americans reported that they would be unable to come up with $2,000 in 30 days if needed.[92]

The cost of health care is a common economic shock. Whereas we could get free medical care if we were poorer, we're now charged for medical care, and U.S. health care is very expensive compared to that of many other countries.[93] Many of us cannot afford health insurance so we often avoid health care until it's urgent.

We have more funds with which to be charitable, and we are actually more proportionately charitable than our wealthier friends.[94] For example, in one experiment, we gave away 40% more of a gift we were to receive to a stranger in need.[95]

We're still juggling, and not just finances: we're juggling money, job duties, family responsibilities, and other everyday life. And, like a physical juggler, we're not really focused on all the balls, just the ones that are about to drop.[96] Whereas the poorest do little negotiating (and have little to negotiate with), we negotiate more. This pays off financially, but it also complicates our life.[97] For example, we often ask for and take advantage of cash discounts, or shop on certain days when the sales discounts are the best.

Our "materiality level," which is the amount of money we think is "a lot," is rising. Whereas at the lowest economic level and at the previous economic level every penny counts, now every dollar counts. Twenty dollars or $100 is a lot of money. This change in our circumstance makes us more likely to ignore small differences in price and begin to pay for convenience. This can be financially dangerous though because small amounts that are incurred very frequently add up to quite a bit of money. So, keeping financially vigilant habits is important. It's also hard. It is easier to do the right thing once than to do so constantly.[98] Convenience matters, even in major decisions we think would be worth for the extra work it takes to earn the convenience premium. For example, studies found that we were 29% more likely to enroll in college when tax professionals not only financially advised us about enrolling in college, but also filled out the forms for us.[99]

Many of us have a bank account, being wage earners for employers who want us to use direct deposit. But, bank accounts require new skills. Unlike paying bills with money orders, using a checking account requires attentiveness to the timing of deposits and withdrawals. Even momentary inattention can be costly to those living on the financial edge, because bounced check fees tend to be high and we often bounce more than one check as a result of a delayed deposit, for example. As such, the skill of anticipating our cash flow is best enhanced by the skill of shopping for a convenient bank with low fees. As we add a savings account, it is easy to add it to the same bank. But, it might be better to put it in another bank that is less convenient for us to reach if we want to keep our money saved. This gives us time to think before spending. While making withdrawals harder, we've also made making deposits to savings harder as well. The cleverest among us may be able to have some money regularly deposited directly from our checking account or income into a passbook-only account, but this requires skill, forethought, and time—and time always seems in short supply.

Marriage makes sense financially because it is no longer the determining factor whether we make too much to receive assistance, and it brings two earners into the family. When one of those is male, statistically that adds more to our household income. And, as our socioeconomic class rises, so does our self-esteem on everything from memory and intelligence, to physical fitness and attractiveness, to honesty and friendliness, to basic skills like cooking and driving.[100] The effects of poverty start in childhood and accumulate over time. The results of being a poor child at age nine continue to affect the brain at twenty-four.[101]

Income and Expenses

For the most part, income is steady enough to support the family, and we work at a rate that might be higher than minimum wage. We might take extra jobs, but only when the money from those jobs is more than the extra cost of childcare, transportation, etc. that come with the extra work. Sometimes our income comes with benefits. Health insurance benefits and sick pay are most important, but having a paid vacation is nice, too.

While we have income, we tend to spend it all over the course of a year. There are good reasons for this. First, we have very little financial cushion if something goes wrong. Second, everyday expenses cost about what we make. Third, there's not a good way to protect our assets even if we could accumulate them, and the assets tend to make very little in interest or other investment return. Yet, we know the importance of living at least a bit below our means, and the concept of saving for a rainy day becomes the norm.

We know that savings can be important to transcend to the middle-middle class. Even when we don't save, our spending will shift toward moving to safer neighborhoods with better schools. We begin buying nonperishable items like toilet paper in bulk to save money over the long term. We begin to purchase select assets that help us save, like tools and laptops. We do begin to add luxuries like children's extracurricular activities. Whereas the impoverished often view philanthropy as working for nothing, or as a rip-off that is sometimes associated with court sentences or punishment, our view of charity evolves into a way to make the world a better place with our time and money.

We continue to manage our expenses by looking for sales, clipping coupons, and expanding our skill set so that we can perform our own repairs and other services rather than paying someone else to do these things. When we do have a skill, we often help those we know for free, and expect them to do the same for us.

Assets and Liabilities

We accumulate a minor amount of assets, storing them where they can be preserved for use in future periods, and our time horizons, which is how far down the road we look and plan, become longer. As the economic dynamic changes, our behavior needs to change. We will buy a freezer, but generally not stocks and bonds, and that's smart in a way because the ability to buy in bulk with a cost savings of 25% for example, well exceeds the return on the market. The return is certain, although not large in dollars, and it is tangible. We shop ahead for items on sale and weigh the cost of layaway because money is tight and credit cards can be a trap, though layaway can be a thoughtful way to secure specific pricey items for the near future. And this forward-looking perspective is an important change from when we were poorer. We now plan for our future in weeks and months, even if it is a relatively short-term future.

Even so, we *are* accumulating assets, especially those that save us money or help us make or protect our income. We may have many several distinct financial instruments at one time.[102] Most of them are very liquid and short-term, though. Those of us that are even moderately tech savvy use tools like the AICPA's 360 degrees of financial literacy[103] website for relatively unbiased and free budgeting tools and savings tips. We like the advice but are leery of someone trying to sell us something.

In most wealthy nations, our work history means that we have some amount of promised benefits, such as the national pension like Social Security benefits promised. How much we need and how we plan to get there is probably vague. Still, we aspire to save for our pensions.

We might aspire to own a house (especially if we are willing to live outside of a city), but are likely still renting. Renting comes with advantages, though. We have the flexibility to move to a cheaper unit or live with family or friends if we hit hard times. We can apply for a housing subsidy if we need one. If we do have a house, we consider renting out extra rooms.

We see more entrepreneurship springing up, like barber shops and rural stores. But, these businesses are often home based or service businesses that normally require little investment and are often operated on a cash basis. We dream of college or trade school education and begin to see them an investment in the future, if we can afford them. Educational scholarships, grants, and loans might be more accessible than we realize, but we must be careful to avoid predatory educational institutions who care more about their own profit than our education.

We may begin saving to own a home, and there are tools to help us. For example, there are Individual Development Accounts (IDAs), which are meant to support the savings goals of our lower-income families. These accounts provide matching for our savings. For every dollar saved in one of these accounts, we receive an additional dollar (or more). Generally, these accounts must be used for education, job training, home ownership, or to fund a small business. Education is provided to strengthen our budgeting and saving skills. As of 2018, over 85,000 IDAs had been opened over the last decade.[104]

Savings is essential if we want to retire. Few of us have a retirement account, and for those of us who do, the average is less than $20,000.[105] This is especially scary because even if our employer has promised to fund a pension for us, they commonly break that promise through a corporate restructuring.

Having more assets does make us happier, but only to the extent that it alleviates financial stress.[106] Betsey Stevenson and Justin Wolfers[107] found that, regardless of country, the more wealth we have, the happier we are. And, the rate of change in happiness was fairly constant, meaning that the satisfaction of moving from the poorest levels to a moderately poor level was about the same as moving from the low end of the upper class to the middle of the upper class. But there's a catch: we must use that money to alleviate financial stress. If instead we invest our happiness in having enough toys and other nonessential material possessions, we are setting ourselves up for more unhappiness.[108] This outlook can be especially problematic at the lower economic levels.

Edward Diener explains that, "if you're poor, it's very bad to be a materialist; and if you're rich, it doesn't make you happier than nonmaterialists, but you almost catch up."[109] Psychologists are uncertain of what causes this relationship. Perhaps attention to material goods takes away time from relationships with family and friends.[110] Marsha Richins theorizes that materialists have unrealistically high expectations of how much happiness material goods can bring.[111] Some psychologists believe that materialistic values may stem from early insecurities, where people use materialism to adapt to having grown up in poor social situations like being mistreated by parents, extreme poverty, or threat of death.[112] Still, it's not the money that causes unhappiness, but the emphasis on money and the striving for material goods.[113]

Worse, some of us are tempted to borrow for unnecessary material possessions. We are just now getting access to credit, but it's expensive. Businesses offering payday loans and other predatory loans advertise to us, but those loans can be very difficult to pay off. For example, payday loans are a $46 billion industry[114] that offers quick access to money on a short-term basis. However, the interest rates on those loans, when calculated on a yearly basis, can be 300% or more, making them among the most expensive loans legally offered, and offered to those of us with the least ability to pay them. We then have to borrow again to pay off those loans and can easily end up in a downward spiral of debt. Some of these loans come with an automatic debit feature, where the lenders debit our bank accounts, sometimes sending us into overdraft status, where we incur overdraft fees in addition to the high interest rates.

On average, half of online payday borrowers were charged $185 in penalties per loan.[115] These loans are generally not spent frivolously. The reason we borrow is poverty itself.[116]

There are used car lots with high interest rates and "rent to own appliance and furniture stores," which incorporate high interest rates into their price. Where we are able to borrow against a car or house, the underlying asset is pledged and presumed to be stable in value relative to the remaining note payable. This means that the balance due on the note goes down faster than the decrease in the asset's fair market value, so that if it's repossessed and resold, the lender does not take a loss.

Credit cards used to be hard to get, but in 1996, the Supreme Court weakened state usury laws that protected us from high interest rates and fees, making our segment of the market more profitable. Now credit cards are more available, but at terms that are usually disadvantageous to us. Missed credit card payments mean a poor credit score, which then means no car loans or home purchases in the next few years. Poor credit scores might also mean being excluded from jobs and inability to rent from a private landlord. Still, with the increased availability of credit, our debt has ballooned. We may take on disadvantageous debt for several reasons, including our youthful inexperience, living beyond our means, or legitimate financial shocks. Still, using this credit may be preferable to the psychic cost of strained relationships when we borrow from friends and family.

Self-employment is more prevalent, but it generally results in more debt.[117] To be successful, we might need to borrow, but we must then be very clear why we are borrowing, how much we can afford, what happens if we default.

To summarize, we survive in this socioeconomic class by staying healthy and staying employed. Medical problems can cause us to miss work, and since we're often paid hourly, also cause us to lose a paycheck. Additionally, there are the medical bills themselves, which draw down our assets and run up our liabilities. Staying employed is crucial, because there's just so very little excess to work with. And, while we're tempted to spend on convenience items, it's not a good strategy for moving up. Working the sales and coupons to save money and shopping at thrift shops and accepting hand-me-downs are good, profitable habits for us. When we need to borrow, borrowing from our network of friends will likely get us better terms than using banks, stores or other businesses; provided they don't habitually borrow as much or more from us on a regular basis. We have some credit available to us now. We learn to make good debt choices.

Small Business Entrepreneurship

Having a small business complicates our banking relationship because to run a successful business, we usually have to have a business account that is separate from our household money. Then, there's more account balances to keep track of, and two sets of expenditures to plan for. We add to our own household money by setting ourselves an informal salary.

That is, we must estimate the total flow of money for the business and household, and gauge how much money flows in between the two. And, we must know if the balance of money is increasing in the business and household accounts between the beginning and end of each period. We must account for the seasonality of our business: what are usually the most and least profitable months? We must estimate profits and estimate tax liabilities in order to make good business decisions. These new skills take vigilance, planning and talent, and the continuous financial pressure itself often hurts our ability to make good decisions. One researcher shared the story of rag collectors in a poor nation who rented their cart for $5 to $10 per month rather than saving and buying one for $30. Clearly, the cost of a cart pays for itself quickly, but "even when returns are high, the poor, who need those returns more than anyone, fail to invest in ways that cannot be explained by weak financial institutions or a lack of skills."[118]

It makes sense for us to convert what are large, periodic payments like estimated taxes into several smaller, more frequent payments so that we are not caught short when the larger payment comes due.[119] It also makes sense to save where we can so that if we do make a mistake in allocating between business and household accounts, we can absorb a resulting economic shock.

Learning to Succeed Financially

We need a financial plan, even if it is an informal one. We need financial goals, the skills to make money, the skills to spend it wisely, the skills to begin to save, and the skills to carefully choose debt, including knowing when it is wise to avoid it. This also means planning for longer into the future. We are no longer hand-to-mouth, but we're not far from it either, and part of moving up means setting longer term goals and keeping them in mind while we balance our daily needs. We can no longer fail to save when cash is momentarily abundant, and deadlines are far away. We benefit from reminders to save, especially reminders that are sent near common payday dates. Oddly, abundance and scarcity are often related for us.

With many basic needs satisfied on a regular basis, investments in education (high-skilled labor or university degrees toward professions with high employment and higher earnings potential) are often the best way to raise revenue.

We are shifting out of qualifying for direct government assistance, but in the U.S. we find indirect assistance through federal income tax filings. With limited effort, we can often increase our overall tax refund by using the deduction for an IRA or other qualified retirement plan in conjunction with the Retirement Savings Contribution Credit, or "Savers Credit." This requires setting up and funding a separate pension account if we don't already have one. Funding this account is relatively simple because by using Form 8888, *Allocation of Refund (Including Savings Bond Purchases)*, the funding can be directly allocated from the current year's tax refund if that return is filed and the account is funded by the regular April due date. This does require willpower though, and with so much stress in life, our willpower might be nearly depleted.

For example, Esther Duflo and the National Bureau of Economic Research et al. (2005) performed an extensive field experiment in cooperation with H&R Block. They used an experimental matching program where cash was given immediately and outright during the tax preparation process as an incentive to save for retirement, rather than as a tax credit. The Savers Credit is effective but not as visible a way to get cash and participants elected to save more often and in greater amounts with the matching than with the Savers Credit. The effect of H&R Block's program to split IRAs to increase the Savers Credit (which pre-dates the current IRS Form for refund allocation available to VITA and all other taxpayers) was "at best very modest."[120] The researchers attributed the modest result to factors that they felt were likely influential in pension savings at tax time such as: financial incentives, tax preparer assistance, the opportunity to use part of an income tax refund to save, and easily accessible savings vehicles; although the one-time aspect of matching in this experiment may also have been significant. After their experiment, the law changed to allow all taxpayers the opportunity to use part of their income tax refund to save. The pension deductions and Savers Credit increased the refund immediately if the refund would be deposited directly before the regular tax filing deadline.

That makes saving for retirement by using our tax refund a very good deal when we file early. But, we've learned to be skeptical of banks. As we increasingly use banks, we might be liable for unintentional debt in the form of bank overdrafts, which result in unexpected high fees. While we intend to save; interest and fines may outstrip our savings progress. So, to move up, we need banks, but we also need to be wary and cautious of our interactions with them.

If We Know What Is Needed Why Don't We Do This?

We often don't do what we should because it is contrary to what we learned and what we believe worked at the lower income levels. AND if we had done these things when were poorer, we fear that we would have been worse off. Those fears may be justified, at least in part. Some of the things that are now holding us back are what helped us rise to begin with.

For example, relationships could help us break out or they could keep us stuck in place. Nine times out of ten, people who transcend do so through a relationship like a teacher, counselor, coach or boss.[121] Increasingly, we are huddling together longer, which should give us a financial advantage. For example, A 2017 New York Times article found that about 40% of adults between 22 and 24 years old receive some financial help from their parents, and the amount that they receive on average is about $250 per month.[122] However, to the extent that those who help us are in the same socioeconomic class, they may be reinforcing the very habits and thinking that are holding us back from moving up. They may discourage education because of the cost. As we do accumulate a little money, they may discourage savings and instead encourage our paying more than our share of family expenses.

Individually, we remain scared that there is not enough money. When there is money, it's tempting to purchase beyond what we need. A little luxury relieves stress and makes us feel normal. Maybe spending a lot on luxuries will make us feel more normal, richer, and more confident. It can be a form of denying that while we are beginning to make it, we haven't got it made yet.

Alternatively, we might do just the opposite and hold on to any extra money too tightly, when strategic spending might help us advance. We hold onto the cash rather than the assets, like a freezer if we have room and large food bills that would allow us to shop for bargains to stretch our money further. Maybe we don't invest in the tools that would make us better at our business or job. By holding on to cash when another asset would help us advance, we could be too cheap.

If we do manage the fear well, it can be a real motivator. We will never be this poor again, and we will do better for our children so that they do not have to endure the pain and fear that we did.

How Much, If at All, Should We Change Those Assumptions?

We probably don't want to cut many, if any people out of our lives, but we may be more discerning in supporting them or loaning them money. Is what they're asking for reasonable? Will they put the money to good use? That is, would money solve their problem or only stall the inevitable a bit or even make the problem worse? Would they loan it to us if we needed it? By turning down the most outrageous or impractical requests, we might be saving more for our family, and the needs of our extended family and friends who might need to make more reasonable requests. Just because we have the money, doesn't mean that we must give it to each family member or friend who asks every time. This may be a change in our social contract, but contracts evolve, and our social bonds should be strong enough to adapt. We might adhere to "loving our neighbor as we love ourselves." As we start to rise, can that translate into loaning no more to others that we keep for ourselves in savings each period? Even so, sometimes, "those that came with you can't always go with you," and that's not always bad. Our friends who are not evolving in their financial attitudes can inadvertently hold us back or become a burden on us as they expect us to share all that we have earned when maybe they have not put forth the same effort.

When deciding how to spend our money, we need to be mindful of whether we are spending on a necessity, investing in something that will pay for itself in savings down the road, or something that just makes us happy. If it just makes us happy, we need to be mindful of how happy it makes us, and for how long we are happy. Normally, possessions don't make us very happy for very long. We must be sufficiently self-aware to know whether we are naturally the binger or the miser, and to test whether we can curb those tendencies safely, one decision at a time. This takes conscientiousness and a focus on a slightly longer time horizon.

When this doesn't come easily for us, it is helpful to put the money where we can't readily get at it if we are a binger, or turn some of it over to a significant other or close family member who will spend it better if we are a miser. By having agreed upon family or group goals, the social group that we should listen to might help us stay the course.

How Might We Best Help Those in Need?

U.S. society has a vested interest in investing in our class, at least in the utilitarian sense. As we transcend, we stop taking government assistance, both directly and in the form of earned income tax credit, and we become net income taxpayers in our own right. We are in one of the highest marginal tax rates in the U.S. tax system. Further, as we begin to afford discretionary items, we do spend most of the money, stimulating the overall economy. We start small bank accounts, which reinforce credit unions and smaller banks. We free our social class members from our asking for loans and that allows them to rise faster.

The U.S. government has responded by encouraging employers and employees to set up Individual Retirement Accounts (IRAs) and other pension funds for their employees. Getting employee participation is another story, though. Two researchers, Shiomo Benartzi and Richard Thaler challenge the idea that people make strictly rational choices and have the willpower to carry them out.[123] Instead, they believe that people use heuristics and welcome help with self-control. As an example of this, they found that making participation in employer-sponsored 401(k)s the default in pension participation increases participation significantly.[124] That is, while maintaining that all pension contributions are optional, making a pension plan an "opt out" plan where contributions are automatic absent action on our part resulted in more savings than an "opt in" plan where we only contribute after we take an action. We're swamped. Sometimes we don't act even when it's best for us. Brigitte Madrian and Dennis Shea found for example, that enrollment of new employees with an opt-out plan reached 90%, versus 20% under the previous, opt-in plan.[125] Zvi Bodie and Henriette Prast found that a combination of multiple behavioral biases like habits and the complexity of life cycle savings models often lead to sub-optimal decision making for pensions.[126]

Thaler and Benartzi (2007) discuss education to improve savings rates, but find little evidence that education is effective in increasing participation or savings rates. However, Choi et al. (2005), while offering a single asset allocation and holding the savings rate constant at 2%, were able to increase the participation rate in 401(k)s from 9% to 34% by making the enrollment extremely simple.

Governmental regulation of predatory lenders has also been called for. Many states have instituted protections against predatory lending, but federal government action has been less consistent. In some cases, education loans have been predatory. Unwary students have been encouraged to take out loans for education, often by for-profit educational institutions, that the institution knew or had reason to know would be difficult to repay with the salaries generated by that education. For example, in 2014, the Consumer Financial Protection Bureau sued ITT Educational Services, Inc. for predatory lending practices, saying it would seek restitution for victims, a civil fine and injunctions against the company.[127] ITT subsequently closed. Still, with support from society, it is easier for us to climb the socioeconomic ladder.

CHAPTER 5

Finally, a Little Something for Ourselves—Moving from Lower-Middle Class to Middle-Middle Class

"I worry a lot about taking care of my dependents, all those perfectly ordinary middle-class preoccupations."[128]

The people of this chapter are also common in the U.S., and our number is growing as the income divide has widened over historically normal levels.[129] Nearly nine out of ten of us consider ourselves to be somewhere in the middle class.[130] What does life look like for us here, broadly and financially?

Life at this Level—All the Basics *and* All the Stress

Life at this level is safer. We face fewer external threats than we did when we had less money. Work and achievement begin to replace entertainment and relationships outside of family as the center of our life. The paperwork documenting our life continues to increase. We might begin to write wills, especially when there are minor children to care for. We keep receipts, especially where we are buying new things that have warranties or where the expenditure affects taxes. We keep or have online access to our credit card statements and bank statements along with mortgage statements or written home leases. We save our tax returns for at least three and preferably, seven years.

Without the dragon of poverty breathing down our neck, we begin to pursue our passions and we feel increasingly more successful.[131] We may pick up a hobby or volunteer at our schools, churches, or other organizations more often. We may travel for vacation. We may have a passport.

We are becoming smarter. We are becoming healthier, and that helps relieve stress, for ourselves and those around us.[132] And because illnesses and injuries would have been expensive, we are able to save on those expenses. When we do pay for health costs, we're more likely to cure or heal something sooner, keeping us working and with regular income. We may be working with companies that have wellness benefits that encourage our physical and indirectly, our financial health.

Our households are stabilizing and moving toward just our immediate family. We can afford a small amount of space of our own, but we still have access to loved ones, usually in the vicinity. We tend to think more nationally in scope, subject to our family roots and culture. Our family structure is more stable than when we were poorer, but not as stable as that of our richer friends.[133]

Our jobs are more stable, and some of us are younger and starting (perhaps even professional) careers. A few of us have college degrees. Economic stability begins to prevail absent habitually poor decisions or an economic shock. Recessions and employment often hit us hardest because now we have something to lose, but not enough extra to build a cushion to offset these shocks. As Lawrence Samuel explains, "[t]he rich can afford hard times or can ride them out while the poor are already poor…"[134]

The fear of economic shocks, which are common, leave us anxious. Whether the shock is from increasing instability in income, the sense that we are falling behind our parents' generation, or comparing ourselves to the very rich, we worry. And, at least some of that anxiety is warranted. Our real income adjusted for inflation has generally not gone up, and because inflation has been present over the last several years but raises have not, we may have even lost ground in real purchasing power. It's not that we don't have luxuries like cell phones and flat screen TVs that our parents didn't have, but we may have to work harder to get them and may be trading them for other luxuries like family vacations. Big ticket items, like housing, college, and health care, have actually outpaced inflation and far outpaced our earnings.[135]

We are saving for more long-term goals now like retirement, a home and education, and the concept of return on investment (ROI) becomes important. Using outside financial institutions becomes the norm. That is, we will save, but now the savings must pay us for the sacrifice of not enjoying the money now. Normally, this comes in the form of interest payments, and the interest rates are not particularly high. But, if by saving we can avoid borrowing at expensive rates in the future, we have an implicit ROI that makes the savings worthwhile. We've made our money back indirectly.

We survive here by *protecting*. We protect some sort of job security, keep expenses less than our income, and save for economic shocks. We also have much more access to debt, and that's a game changer. In some areas, access to debt means access to an affordable home mortgage and a loan for a car reliable enough to give us a choice of where we live and what jobs are practically available to us. Access to credit helps protect us from being devastated by economic shocks because we can charge the help that we need and pay it off over time in what are often a series of affordable payments without depleting what we have saved, for example, in pension plans. Credit can become affordable enough to be costly, so costly that we drown in it. Suddenly having to take out credit derails our plans for progress. That is, our financial progress is two steps forward, one step back, rather than linear like we usually plan, and that's discouraging.

While we protect what we have, some of the government protections we were used to when we were poorer are slipping away, which is scary. While our lot has improved since the Great Recession of 2008, it has not improved nearly as much as those of our wealthier friends **or** our poorer friends.[136] Counterintuitively, increases in benefits and social programs, especially medical benefits and tax benefits, have benefitted poorer people but not us. We're losing the Earned Income Tax Credit, so we're working as hard as ever, but increases in salary are offset in part by declining government transfer programs in a way that is not at all straightforward. This comes at the same time that we are being squeezed by our employers to pay more for health insurance and other benefits. We don't know the statistics exactly, but we feel the stagnation. The stagnation is real, as graphed in the tables below. We have tried to do everything right—working and saving—and we are not progressing, but it seems that everyone else is. Even so, if we are still better off by most measures than when we were poor, including measures of income, health, death rates, and incarceration rates.[137]

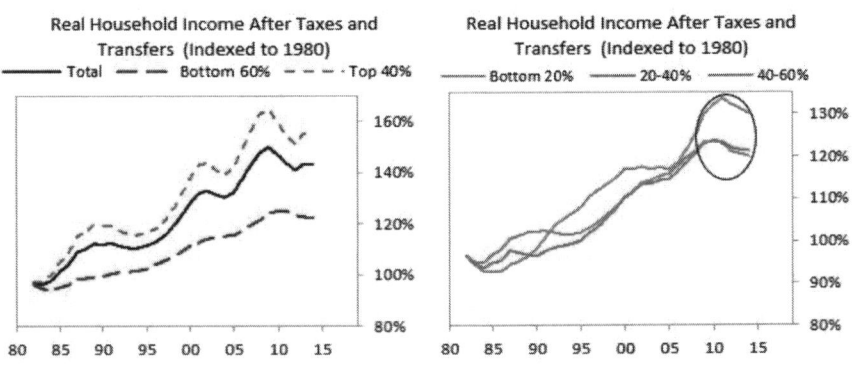

Source: https://www.linkedin.com/pulse/our-biggest-economic-social-political-issue-two-economies-ray-dalio/

Still, there are things, like our jobs, that we just can't protect. We have been hit hard by decline in manufacturing jobs, which were what we were used to seeing growing up. There are more highly skilled jobs which generally require a college education, and more low-skilled jobs that are often not full-time and pay much lower wages. So, we find ourselves needing to work longer hours or retrain just to stay even.[138]

Income and Expenses

Members of our households are more likely to have steady, full-time jobs. Those jobs may be salaried or include provisions for overtime. We often have at least basic benefits including the following: partial sponsorship of health insurance, perhaps with vision or dental benefits, a life insurance policy, possibly a long-term health insurance option, and a pension plan in which we can contribute that the company might match. We might have something called "flex" benefits available, and we might be able to set up one to two savings accounts through the company to be used on an annual basis for childcare or out-of-pocket medical expenses on a before tax basis. We may get paid vacation and/or sick leave. Many of us find the complexity of the benefits available to us baffling, but there's often some help from our employers if we just ask.

Having benefits might complicate our taxes as well. Which are taxable? Which save us taxes? Which have no effect on taxes? If we buy a house, our taxes might become more complicated as well. Can we itemize? If we itemize, then we can deduct charitable contributions as well, but did we get and keep adequate receipts? We still generally get modest tax refunds, but it's difficult to understand why or how those refunds are figured.

Whereas when we were poorer, we needed discipline to get to a dead-end job on time every day, we now have that discipline down and work to keep our expenses in check. We have enough extra money or credit to pursue some passions, but only if we don't passionately overspend. With the introduction of structured credit in our lives, we must also evaluate interest expense features, like variable versus fixed interest rates.

We make cash outlays to protect our income, like buying a car to give us better employment options and maybe a chance to make money with ride sharing on the side. We're still looking to buy things that end up saving us money over the course of a year or more. And, we have more tools as well as more cash to do so. With reliable online internet and a sufficient data plan, we can cautiously search for online savings. The internet also provides us with quick tools to help us make educated choices and give us tips on finances, like how to budget, what types of loans are available, and how they work. There's no treasured degree associated with this education, but when we use it, we can keep from making costly mistakes.

Assets and Liabilities

Getting more education is a possibility especially with scholarships, loans, government grants, and tax breaks. We must determine what kind of education to get, where to get it, and how to pay for it. Done well, this requires a whole new skill set, and we may not get it right on the first try. Deciding on the right education is a personal choice, but we should make that decision with the other factors of where to get the education and how to pay for the education in mind. Simply following our dream without knowing how many jobs are available in our field and what they pay can leave us without a job (if there aren't many in the field) and with a lot of student debt that will follow us for years. We could be worse off, and we generally know someone who is. The school we choose to attend may help us find that information, but often, the school is concerned with admitting enough students or admitting the "right" students than with the economics of our schooling choice. For-profit schools in particular have this reputation.

So where do we begin if we weren't raised by college educated parents who know how to navigate this system advantageously? Many high school guidance counselors have an indication of our what career choices are available and what schools are generally open to people with our high school credentials. If it's been a long time since we've been in high school, we may be more self-aware of what we do and do not like, and how others have become successful (as we define it) and happy. Simultaneously, the Bureau of Labor Statistics lists different jobs, how many jobs are available, and what they pay on average. This information is downloadable into Excel for easier sorting.[139] Backing that up with other data on what the demand will be for future jobs, we can narrow down our choice to just a few careers.

We can then see what the educational and interning requirements are for the jobs we like best or can tolerate, and where we will make more money. The career we choose has a large bearing on whether we go to a trade school or community college, a four-year college, or higher still. Where we do choose a career needing at least a college degree, we could save a substantial amount of money by attending a community college for the first two years of that degree, then transferring to a four-year college, provided we stay motivated on the long-term goal. From the outset, we need to coordinate the education within the two schools so that we are not paying for a lot of community college hours that don't transfer to our desired four-year institution.

Then comes pricing the education, which in itself is tricky. Most schools publicly list their tuition, fees, and cost of attendance for those who are expected to live on a campus. In any case, we should view tuition and required fees together, because some schools have low tuition that is more than offset by higher fees than other institutions. But, public schools, private not-for-profit schools, and private for-profit schools are still not comparable because like bargaining for money off a sticker price on a car, different institutions give different discounts on their posted price in the form of grants and scholarships which do not have to be paid back. So, for example, while public schools usually have a lower tuition "sticker price," not-for-profit schools with high endowments may provide a lower net tuition and fees.

If we work for a college that is part of a tuition exchange system, our own work there may mean that our tuition and fees, but not our room, board, books and supplies, are paid for in all or part. If we are a veteran of the armed forces, state and/or federal benefits might fund our education. If we enlist in the military or ROTC, we may get financial support for college. If we are willing to work in fields like teaching in places where there are few teachers, our loans might be paid for us during the times that we work in those areas. Ultimately, if we are serious about a career, communicating with the financial aid office of each institution we are interested in is essential to estimating our own personal net cost. We also need to be clear about what discounts apply *each* year, and what loans (that will have to be repaid) are included in each institution's educational cost estimates. Having a low-cost freshman year, only to perform well but have much higher tuition and fees in the following year could derail our plans, causing us to quit without the skills for the higher income, but with some student debt for our freshman year. That's just the cost of the degree.

Now comes the cost/benefit analysis. Does paying for the education make financial sense? That is, will this education train us for a career with enough openings that we'll likely get a job, and if so, will we make enough extra money over having no degree to pay for that degree in a reasonable amount of time? Following our dreams into a career as a NASCAR mechanic could be great fun, but if it's very hard to get a job because too many of us want that job relative to the openings that are available, and we're making minimum wage if we do get the job, our prospects for advancing financially are bleak. That's not to say we shouldn't follow our dreams. That's to say that our dream of being a NASCAR mechanic collides head-on with our dream of becoming a millionaire. Our education, which was meant to be an intangible asset that lifts us to the next level, has actually saddled us with more debt than we can pay on our own.

We've seen our friends make those choices and so sometimes we question whether education is still worth it at all. In truth, the answer is, "it depends." If we've considered both the costs and benefits going in, and we understand the loans that we take out (if any), then a carefully considered higher education degree still statistically leads to a higher lifetime income. But, making a mistake on a big-ticket item like higher education can be very costly.

So, once we know what skill to pursue at what institution, we are now challenged by how to make the cash flow work, given that we likely have little cash saved for school. If the degree is for our children, having our children work part-time in high school and over the summer is a help, as is our taking extra work where we can. In some cases, we can work at the school that we attend. This is advantageous but not because of the salary. The schools we work for are normally sympathetic of the academic demands that courses place on us. And, we can network within the university to better navigate the system and to pick up additional learning that in pieces seems inconsequential, but in aggregate makes the degree program easier, as well as gives us a work history and money.

Ultimately, someone in our family is probably taking out student loans that will affect the family for years. To navigate the student loan system, and to make ourselves more eligible for grants and scholarships, the first step is to fill out the Free Application for Federal Student Aid, or "FAFSA" each year prior to our upcoming year's attendance in school.[140] The FAFSA website itself has information on colleges, including a college scorecard for each college with the college costs, graduation rate, and post-college earnings. To complete the FAFSA, we may need our most recent tax return. After we complete the FAFSA, we will get an estimated cost of college, the amount of any government grants, and the amount for which we can get a government loan. There are often also private loans available to students and parents. Together with scholarships, what we can save from working, and any assets we may have already saved for college, we can put together a plan to pay for college while still meeting our own personal and family responsibilities.

In a perfect world, the best student loans are loans taken out by the student, not the parent, because the parent's retirement and/or ability to afford a home could be compromised by the student's unpaid loans. The student generally has longer to earn money to pay off loans than the parent. Government loans often do not require a parent to cosign but requiring a cosigner is common among private lenders, and with private lenders, there are often less protections after college if we can't pay back this loan. Some student loan interest is deferred and does not add to the balance due until after we've graduated. Obviously, this is better for us than student loans that accrue interest while we are still in college. And, interest rates on student loans vary, so shopping loans is a must for our financial health.

Taken together, while we desire higher education and begin to see its value, given the choice between investing in a higher education and investing in a home, most of us prefer to buy a home. Buying a home makes sense over the long run for many of us in areas where homes are affordable. We still have a monthly cash outflow like we were leasing, but some of that outflow goes to pay off the principal balance on the home, so that we have an asset to sell when we want to move rather than having no asset were we to rent.

The mortgage interest and some of the property tax portion of owning a home are tax deductible if we itemize deductions on our tax return, though most of us don't have enough deductions to make that worthwhile. So, indirectly, housing costs may go down over the cost of leasing. But, we are responsible for repairing and maintaining the home, and for older homes, this cost could give rise to unpleasant financial surprises.

To buy a home, we need a down payment. Normally we save for one, and the amount of the down payment needed to buy a home is negotiated between buyer, lender, and seller. Down payments of 10–20% are common, and the larger the down payment, the better the loan terms tend to be. As a buyer, there are usually few closing costs added to the loan, but one common closing cost is "points." A point is one percent of the loan value, and each point serves to buy down the interest rate that's paid on the remainder of the loan. That is, when we shop with multiple lenders for a home loan, knowing the interest rate is not enough, we need to know the points that will be charged at closing, and whether we can afford them in addition to the down payment. We also need to be cautious of monthly payment quotes, which sometimes include only principal and interest, not the lender-required insurance and government required property taxes. While the insurance and property taxes are generally paid yearly, most lenders require that we pay an estimated amount for these bills in our monthly payments in addition to principal and compound interest on our home loan. Most mortgage companies put these extra payments in an escrow account, so that if we've overpaid, our monthly payments will be less next year.

With a house comes long-term responsibility and the need for stable income, especially if we also have children in the home. So, we think about life insurance. There are many insurance salespeople ready to sell us a policy, which means we need yet another skill set. How much insurance do we need and what kind of policy should we buy? If we are lucky enough to have insurance at work of at least one times our annual salary, that is a good start. The amount of that insurance might be enough. If we have no children, we only need enough to pay our bills and bury us when we die. If we have children, then we need to increase the amount by the amount to provide for the children until they reach an age of independence. Normally, term life insurance is the cheapest and best value for us because saving money that is not offset with high life insurance commissions is paramount to where we are financially, and because we expect our need for life insurance to fall off as our children age and our retirement accounts grow.

Our jobs might provide us with a way to save for our retirement through structured payroll deductions. In some cases, the employer matches our contributions, and in a few rare cases, our employer funds retirement for us. A beautiful thing about these plans is, employer matching or funding seems free to us, and what we contribute to our retirement savings generally escapes income tax now. We might be able to make contributions to Individual Retirement Accounts (IRAs) and receive a tax deduction this year, or make a "Roth" IRA contribution, which does not give us a tax deduction this year but allows us to withdraw the balance of the account tax-free when we retire. But now comes a new question, where do we invest this money?

Bank instruments like certificates of deposit (CDs) are an easy answer. They're safe, but the interest rate on those accounts is often less than inflation, which means that while the nominal amount of the account is increasing, what that amount of money can buy is actually decreasing. The return on investment for mutual funds is historically higher and a better choice for the long term. However, these accounts can experience losses. During good times, the returns are much higher than in a bank account, but during bad times, the account balances actually fall. And, which mutual fund should we buy? The choices are overwhelming. Many mutual fund houses now offer easy choices where they professionally assemble a set of funds around our estimated retirement year. With a retirement fund and Social Security, we may be able to retire if our debts are paid off.

But, odds are, we have more debt than our poorer friends. Our ability to borrow greatly increases as unsecured credit cards are available to us for the first time. Credit must be managed for the first time, because prior to this, any limited credit we could get was tightly managed by the lender. We might actually have our choice of credit cards, so we're not only looking for low interest rates and no annual fee, we might have to analyze cash back opportunities on credit cards. And these complications double if we also face these same questions with a small business that we own.

Small Business

Our business financial life is also more complicated. Different elements of the financial statements are now intertwined, and we need more education to understand and maximize our finances. Take hair styling for example, we might be moving up from renting space at a hairdressing shop to owning the hair dresser shop and renting out space. We have more bills to pay, larger bills to pay, and more sources of revenue to keep straight. We might also have access to a line of credit. We might want to save for expansion of our business.

The IRS offers videos to help us.[141] The Small Business Administration website[142] offers updated financial tools for entrepreneurs. They are also a source for small business loans.

We need a business education, even if it's in the form of rules of thumb.[143] Some key lessons are:

1. Understanding the basics of accounting: why it's relevant, and how to estimate cash accumulation and profits using itemized records

2. Understanding personal/household income and expenses, and how they affect the business; daily records to estimate profit daily and weekly profits (and the time period extends as we grow richer); fixed costs, and how they affect profit

3. Aggregating daily records into monthly records; monthly profit; accounts payable, accounts receivable

We Want More

To be happier, we may need to spend less. We may need to **replace** the "if I had more money and more things, I wouldn't be unhappy" thinking, because that used to be true, but once a certain income level is reached, materialism does not make us happier and may make us more discontent. That is, money can buy some happiness, especially more than if we were poor, but the pursuit of money for materialistic purposes actually buys us unhappiness, and that concept is new to us.

Because our jobs are changing, our understanding of work must change as we want our income to continue to increase. Whereas we were likely paid hourly with few benefits or overtime when we were poorer, we are more likely to be salaried and have better jobs to protect. This may mean working longer hours with no immediate reward, so the ability to look at delayed gratification and a longer time period is crucial. Our jobs may not begin and end on a strict timetable. We may have to come in early, work late, or work on scheduled days off to do our jobs properly, but we may receive paid vacation, paid sick leave, and possibly receive flextime, where working off our regular schedule is compensated by time off during the regular work week.

For example, one woman who previously worked at an hourly position in a day care facility decided to alter her career and become a nanny. The pay was about the same, but there was free housing, food, and travel that significantly sweetened the pot and her upward mobility. However, that required a radical shift to fit into a different established culture. Her employer would say something like, "I need you until about 6 tonight." Six o-clock passed, and the employer was still in a meeting that didn't end until about 6:30. The nanny was impatient, interrupted the meeting so that she could leave at 6, and when she was still needed, wanted overtime immediately. The employer thought of 6 as an estimate, believed the business meeting was more important than precision on what time the day ended, but was willing to offset the extra time with more time off later at a mutually agreeable time. In short, the employee thought it was her job to work certain hours, the employer thought her job was to add value to the household which required new flexibility. Arguably, the employee didn't understand her real job, and ultimately it cost her that position.

We begin planning for an increasingly longer term as we are increasingly more successful, and that requires more short-term self-discipline. Previously, it was easy to not spend money because we *didn't* have any. Now we can spend what we have. With credit, we can also financially misbehave on a large scale.

We need new skills for handling debt that wasn't particularly relevant when we were poorer when no one gave us credit. Educating ourselves on top of meeting all the other demands of our stressed life is difficult. We might need to know how to shop for car loans and or mortgage loans. We need to understand how debt payments affect principal and interest expense. We need to understand what an escrow is and how it is reconciled. In seasons when money is scarce, we need to know how to prioritize debt payments, and that's not something that we have much experience with. In fact, we rarely prioritize the debts with the highest late fees or interest rates.[144] That makes sense where our assets are pledged and can be repossessed and resold if we default. Still, when we have several unsecured debts due, we often pay the debt with the largest balance only to incur late payment fees and demerits to their credit rating on several bills, not just one.[145]

Those of us with higher credit scores are more likely to consider debt.[146] We need rules of thumb as to when to take on debt. We also need a skill set for deciding where to borrow, and we need to know what safety nets are available if we are in danger of defaulting on those loans.

Some key takeaways for us are:

1. When the minimum payments on all debts can be made, pay extra on those with highest interest rates first.

2. When the minimum payments on all debts is not possible, pay secured debt first (home mortgages, car notes, etc.), because the repossession on those items is often swift and disruptive.

3. Protect our credit scores by paying debts that don't drop off a credit report after seven years, like unpaid tax liens, child support arrears, and student loans in default.

Where times are particularly bleak, it might make sense to make no payment rather than a very small one. Six months after a last payment, most lenders write-off the debt by selling it to a collection agency. The collection agency can only pursue the unpaid debt for a limited number of years, a number which is set by each state. Most credit card debts fall off a credit report 7 years after the last payment. So, credit card companies and debt collectors are motivated to "both hassle and make accommodations" for those of us willing to continue making payments of any amount.[147] In the worst cases, we would declare bankruptcy, but ironically, we can't afford to. This adds to our financial stress and creates fear.

We also often give lower priority to debts that we perceive are not fully legitimate, like where a creditor is seen to be charging too high of an interest rate or we feel has been fraudulent.[148] We consider cards with hidden fees, fines, and high interest following low "teaser" rates to be less legitimate, and these debts get paid last. If years of meeting minimum monthly payments leaves the balance owed largely unchanged, as with "interest only" payment terms, we view those debts as less legitimate.

When a large debt payment is made, it often comes because we've received our tax refund. This is an opportune time to make substantial progress on debt, and when we do this, we cut debt by an average of 50%.[149] However, a plan that allows us to fall behind on debt only to make it up at tax time is not a sound one. It hurts our credit scores and we incur late fees. Education on how to make these choices is available and free resources are available to many of us. However, few of us seek out help or information on resolving debt. We just don't know about these services or where to look for them.[150]

Why We Might Not Do More

We don't do it in part because it is contrary to what we learned and believe to have worked at the lower levels, and if we were to do these things when we were poorer, we would have been worse off. For example, we fear applying for credit, even when we need it.[151] Those fears may be justified, at least in part.

We fear that we don't have enough liquid savings to last very long if we lose our job or have an economic shock like if our car breaks down. How can we save for retirement if we're not sure we've saved for what could happen next month? What if I borrow thousands for an education and then can't find a job in my new field? What if I buy a house, then lose my job? What if I set up a savings account, but it's eaten away by bank fees? What if I invest in a mutual fund and the stock market crashes? What if I get a credit card and then over-spend? These are all valid fears. But, these fears stop us from moving forward. Maybe we can test how valid these fears are by making small, safe changes.[152]

How Much, If at All, Should We Change Those Assumptions?

While asking how we can save for retirement if we're not sure we've saved for what could happen next month, we can put a small amount away for retire-ment automatically from our paychecks. If we're not hurt, we can increase that amount yearly or as part of every raise that we receive.

What if I borrow thousands for an education and can't find a job in my new field? We can confine our borrowing to government and other loans that have a safety valve if we are unable to repay the loan, and we can choose a skill or college major that we have researched independently of what schools recommend ensuring that there are generally well-paying jobs in the field. We can ask if there is a cheaper way to get an education. For example, can we get some of our needed courses at community college, which tends to be cheaper, and transfer the credit hours in to a more expensive institution if further education is needed?

What if I buy a house, then lose my job? The results may not be markedly different than if we were to lose a job while leasing an apartment. Then again, we might be able to renegotiate the loan or refinance with the lender.

Instead of asking, what if I set up a savings account, but it's eaten away by bank fees, we can ask, "can I find a credit union that has lower fees and is more customer oriented?"

If our question is,: "what if I invest in a mutual fund and the stock market crashes?," I might invest only with large, reputable funds that I think would have government bailouts if their institution fails. When we invest with more than one institution our investment is safer because the odds of one institution failing is low, and the odds of two institutions failing is lower still.

What if I fear that if I get a credit card I will overspend? I might get a debit card until I'm sure that I have developed good habits. Also, I might get a credit card with a low credit limit that I know that I can pay off without too much trouble.

How Might We Best Help Those in Need?

Policymakers could, and sometimes do address the low savings rate in the U.S. The U.S. credit and banking system makes it easy for unsophisticated consumers to worsen our finances. Many credit card companies offer contracts with absurdly low minimum payments, which induces some of us to <u>incur large penalties</u> for not paying off the full amount. Consumer protection agencies could change the rules, for instance, raising minimum payments for most customers.[153]

Many companies don't have 401(k)s, or they make us opt-in to contribute. Companies might not adequately explain the benefits of putting away more money, or they make it easy for us to draw down our balances at will. These policies "nudge" us to be bad savers. The U.S. could change the default settings for qualified retirement plans or allow Americans to save more through expanded Social Security.[154]

CHAPTER 6

A Steady Job, A Good Neighborhood, and Team Sports for the Kids— Moving from Middle-Middle to Upper-Middle Class, Life in the Upper Half of the Spectrum

"...[T]hey do most of the working and paying and living and dying in this community. Well, is it too much to have them work and pay and live and die in a couple of decent rooms and a bath?"[55]

Most of us identify as being middle class, "average Americans" even when statistically we're in a different net worth category.[156] This might be in part because when we're poor, we know people who are even poorer still and so we feel wealthier (but not rich), and when we're rich, we know people who are wealthier still, so we do not feel wealthy.

Life at this Level—From Fear of Deprivation to Fear of Stagnation

What does life look like for us, broadly and financially? We are increasingly more literate as our income rises.[157] We have fewer immediate threats to our safety and welfare. We are psychologically better off than when we were poorer, in part because we have less stress.[158] We place less emphasis on clothing, entertainment, food, jail, housing, and safety, and more time thinking about shopping, hobbies and sports, retirement, education, prevention, and political action.[159] We have smaller households that cluster around primary family units, and less of a social need for community and church. We may have travelled to several states, and even internationally on a limited basis. It is easier to stay in touch electronically because our phones are not turned off by providers and we have email and social media available to us if our phones do fail us. If an unexpected need arises, we might be able to crowd fund a solution.

We continue to be anxious, but the anxiety is changing. Worry about jobs becomes worry about careers. Worry about children becomes worry about childcare. Worry about getting by becomes worry about not doing as well as our parents' generation and never being Kardashian-rich.[160]

We feel that we increasingly have more control over our lives. We spend longer hours at the office, and we are increasingly more likely to keep a job we dislike for financial reasons. We begin keeping more complex records, like receipts. We often spend evenings on undergraduate or graduate courses, and our student debt grows. Our household is run on a budget and our time is budgeted and planned out in advance. This extra effort often pays off. We outsource repairs like plumbing and electric work. High quality clothes, shoes, furniture, and cars become affordable. We contribute to charity with both our time and money. Our children are in structured extracurricular activities like little league, piano lessons, swim team, etc. We can afford yearly vacations if we plan in advance. Our disposable income is small, but it's there, and our wants grow with our income. We have a credit card, and while we may use it cautiously, we're not afraid to use it.[161]

Income and Expenses

We have income from more sources as we get wealthier. We have a salary or good hourly wage and we also likely have benefits. We have some savings for retirement and short-term needs, and those assets should earn an income independent of our day job. We can expect a bigger pension from Social Security. If we get extra money, we're more likely to spend it on something we want than to save it, especially if we did not have much notice that we were receiving the money.

Our income is more likely to come with important, but confusing benefits. Flexible spending arrangements (FSAs) reduce our take-home pay in the short run but save us money in the long run. FSAs are normally offered for both childcare and health care costs, although when we want both, our employer will keep these two accounts separate for us. What comes out of paycheck for these accounts is subtracted before the government imposes income tax on it, meaning that when we do use it for childcare or health care, we are paying with before tax dollars. Another way to think about this is, the government never taxes what we put into this account provided that we use it as intended. If we do not contribute to these accounts, we pay for childcare and health care *and* we pay income taxes on these bills. While we get out of income tax on FSAs, we do have to pay Social Security and Medicare tax on this money.

Because our income is stable, we can generally pay for our everyday living expenses without too much trouble, but non-recurring expenses such as medical expenses and car repairs are difficult for us. And, with the increasing pace with which we are living our life, it easy for us to ignore recurring expenses even though outside circumstances have slowly changed. So, we miss the opportunity to renegotiate these bills downward or eliminate them altogether to save a few dollars a month, which works out to be hundreds of dollars per year.

Yearly income tax becomes a factor for perhaps the first time. At lower levels of income, we received the Earned Income Tax Credit. Now, that's essentially disappeared. We may owe money after a major life change like marriage, divorce, or having children grow up and leave home.

We are able to help our children reach their dreams by paying for at least part of their college, but we may have to make a choice to reduce or borrow against our retirement funds. Because we love our children so much, it's tempting to sacrifice our retirement funds at least in part for our children. Indeed, the more support that we can give our children, generally the less debt that the family has and the better off our children are. However, the children have more time to pay off student loans than we have time to replace retirement savings. And, parents can't borrow for retirement as easily as children can borrow for college. So, it is often better to ask our children to work while in college, and where possible, live at home while in college. Some children will opt to get college benefits from the military.[162]

Assets and Liabilities

As income rises, our sources of income can and should diversify. While it was important that our savings be safe and earn a bit, return on investment is more important as we earn more. We are building asset portfolios. Short-term savings, retirement savings, some college savings, life insurance, and home ownership are the most common elements of our asset portfolio. This is a natural diversification of assets and committing to diversification is important for our upward mobility. For the first time, we look at managing what longer-term *wealth* we have, not just our income and expenses. And, because we have more assets to manage, it is naturally more complicated. To make it easier to save for each goal, we probably have different "mental accounts" for each goal and may have different physical accounts for each savings goal. We normally have a different physical account for retirement than we do for other kinds of savings, if only to maximize the tax benefits. Even if we have just one other savings account, in our mind or in an Excel ledger where we keep track of our accounts, we have a goal for vacation savings, a goal for economic shocks, a goal for holiday spending, a goal for big ticket items like cars and house down payments, and maybe a goal for higher education savings. We contribute as we can to each of these goals. As each goal is reached, we divert additional contributions to the other goals we want to fund. If all our savings goals are reached, we often spend extra money rather than accumulate more.[163]

There are also new threats to our assets but sometimes they're subtle. There are new ways to defraud us, and a new, less overt kind of spoilage for our long-term assets—inflation. Now, we want to make our assets earn as much as inflation plus a bit more over the long term. That's difficult because that almost certainly means beginning to invest in the stock market or other vehicles beyond bank savings accounts, and those are subject to shifting economic conditions that are difficult for us to understand and impossible for us to consistently predict or control.

Take retirement savings. We may save regularly, but how much should we save? We understand that what we save will earn interest, dividends, or capital gains, but how much will it earn, net of tax? And, all the answers to these questions depend on when we start saving and how much we expect to make shortly before we retire, not necessarily what we make now. In one study, researchers showed that a 35-year-old couple with household income of $50,000 needs to save about 11% to 13% pre-tax to maintain their lifestyle in retirement; that same couple with household income of $100,000 would need to save 13% to 17% using 2017 data.[164] That's more than most of us can afford, and that's just for retirement savings.

The researcher's estimate is based on low predicted future investment returns. Low returns reduce the amount that our asset balances earn, and those lower earnings extend into retirement. We may need that retirement longer, because advances in medicine help us live longer and healthier while we are in retirement. That's good news, but that means that our savings have to stretch over a longer period of time. Retiring later, at age 70 or 72, lowers the percentage that we need to save. For instance, a single 35-year-old person with household income of $50,000 who wants to retire at 60 needs to save 19.1% per year to fund their desired lifestyle in retirement, or 15.8% if they want to retire at 65, or 10.6% if they want to retire at 70.[165]

With decisions becoming more complicated, it makes sense to work with a well-recommended financial planner. These planners often work on commission, which is to say that we can get advice without paying money out of our pocket. We are still paying them, but we are paying them indirectly, which preserves our cash flow. Often our bank will have financial planners, and if we do have a mutual fund, often our mutual fund house will have financial planners that we can talk to. It's important to remember that while we are not paying financial planners directly, they do not have to sell us the products that are best for us. So, it's best to interview two or three recommended financial planners before investing with one.

Financial planners might recommend mutual funds, which is a pre-built, professionally managed share in a diversified stock portfolio. Financial planners might recommend that we build a "bond ladder," which is a series of bond purchases that mature sequentially during our retirement years. When we purchase safe bonds[166] and hold them to maturity, we know what the return on investment will be. However, when the bonds mature, we generally end up spending both the principal and the interest, which hurts us financially if we live past the retirement age that we planned for.

A financial planner might recommend that we purchase annuities. An annuity is a contract, generally with an insurance company or investment company. The terms of annuities vary, but annuities can be funded with one lump sum or through a series of contributions. Normally, these contributions are made with after-tax savings, but then the investment grows tax free until we begin to take withdrawals. Normally, the investment pays out after a set time in a series of equal payments equally spaced in time, consisting of part non-taxable principal and part taxable interest. Payouts can be for a fixed period of time or for a lifetime. Sometimes the annuity also has an insurance feature in case of premature death. While annuities can at times be very afford-able and flexible, they can also come with high fees and commissions, so it's important to shop options across two or three financial planners.

In the alternative, we might consider retiring in phases, where we work part-time, maybe on a flexible or seasonal basis. Increasingly, more Americans are choosing this option.[167] This option is attractive if we are also helping to pay for our children's higher education expenses.

So, how do we save for both retirement and our children's college? Clearly, it's not easy, and having a college account separate from retirement and general savings is probably best. To keep from raiding that account for our everyday emergencies, it's best to have an account which is hard to access or withdraw from. We might set up an automatic bank transfer to that account every month using online banking. There are also special, dedicated savings accounts called "529 plans"[168] that allow our savings to grow without tax until we withdraw them. If we withdraw the funds to pay qualified higher education expenses, the earnings on those funds are never taxed. If our first child does not choose a higher education path, the account can be transferred to other relatives for their education and will still be tax free. A downside to these funds is that sometimes the seller imposes high, up-front fees for the first few years on these accounts, and after accounting for the time value of money, it may be cheaper in the long run to set up a regular account and pay taxes on the earn-ings than to commit to high, up-front commissions. An alternative to 529 plans is investing in U.S. Savings bonds. This technique is not in vogue, but it's tried and true. We can use it to save several small amounts like $25 very regularly. It is less attractive to raid for other purposes and can be attractive when interest rates are near historical norms. The income on Series EE savings bonds, if used for education, is tax-exempt. However, the interest rate on these bonds has recently been very low.

It's also useful to research every possible education benefit that our children might qualify for. For example, unused Texas veterans' education benefits can be passed down to dependents to provide up to 150 hours of tuition and fees at most public Texas college and universities.[169]

Let's face it, we don't know if our children will get into college or want to go, or even if it will be what is best for them. So, we might choose to invest in a 401(k) or Roth 401(k) at work or Roth IRA above what we would normally invest for our retirement. That way, to the extent that our children receive scholarships or other funding, the retirement money can be used to fund a better retirement. To the extent that we do fund college, we may be able to borrow against the 401(k), or withdraw a Roth. Withdrawals on Roth accounts are both taxed and penalized if withdrawn before we turn 59½.

Second only to purchasing a home, a college education is likely the most expensive purchase that many of us will have. Student loans have become increasingly problematic for us, although defaults on student loans are decreasing.[170] In 2017, the average balance outstanding was $34,144, which was up 62% and the percentage of borrowers who owe $50,000 or more has tripled over the last 10 years.[171]

We can also borrow against our home with a home equity loan to pay for college if need be. However, that might indirectly upset our ability to retire on schedule because we will now have another house note, where before we had only one mortgage or the house may have been paid off entirely, lowering our monthly bills and need for income in our retirement years. Also, by having a home mortgage interest, there's less of a safety net should we want to take out a reverse mortgage in retirement. These loans may come with either fixed or variable rates. With fixed rates, we know the amount of the required payment, and that amount generally won't change until the loan is paid off. However, that certainty comes with a price—fixed interest rates are often higher than variable interest rates. And, while variable interest rates can go up and down, they often come with a "collar" so that that they won't go up or down more than an amount specified in the contract. After December 31, 2017, the interest that is paid on this loan is generally not tax deductible.[172] If it's deductible, it's an itemized deduction, so we only benefit if we have enough expenses to file Schedule A, *Itemized Deductions*, with our tax return. There are some traps to using home equity financing. Some lenders advertise artificially low "teaser" rates which increase after one to three years unless the loan is paid off in full.

Regardless of how we save, where do we get the money to save? One of the most effective ways to save is by saving a little at a time as the money comes in, like with a payroll deduction that is automatically diverted to a savings account, investment account, or bond purchase. A variation on that savings plan is to save a little at a time with every purchase. There are "round up" apps that take a purchase of, for example, $23.46 and round it up to $24.00, with the extra $0.54 being swept into a savings account. It is the equivalent of having a spare change bowl at home, where the balances add up so painlessly over time, that they're largely forgotten.

Another effective source of savings are tax refunds and tax rebates, which may be the single biggest cash payment we receive during the year. Two researchers[173] studied responses to hypothetical lump sum tax rebates of the size distributed in 2008, $300 and $600. The government granted these rebates to stimulate the economy. The researchers found that for amounts under $600, we were likely to spend a rebate if the government wanted us to spend it, but at or above $600, the government's wishes were ignored, and we saved a substantial percent of it.

Where we receive more regular, estimable payments, some of us build those payments into the budget, but some of us don't. Hsieh found that people receiving bonuses from the Alaska Permanent Fund built it into their budget, summarizing that, "households will take anticipated income changes into account ...when the income changes are large, regular and easy to predict."[174] However, two other researchers, Browning and Collado, found no effect to our spending when they studied semi-annual Spanish bonuses.[175]

Where we do save lump sum payments like tax refunds, they're often saved for short-term goals and used up before the end of the year. We can increase our chance of making saving long-term by planning in advance to earmark future cash inflows and moving at least some of those inflows to accounts that are inconvenient for us to access. We might not fully achieve our goals, but statistically, we will come closer than if we don't set a goal, plan for how we will achieve it, and put external controls into place.

We are more likely to borrow than we were when we were poorer. Unlike our poorer selves, to become richer we sometimes should borrow. We begin to build credit portfolios consisting of multiple credit cards and notes. Like an asset portfolio, our credit portfolio needs to be managed. It even results in a credit score which is essential to our ability to borrow as is advantageous to us.

When Should We Borrow?

We should consider borrowing when in the long run, it increases our income or decreases our expenses, by more than the interest rate we are charged. Doing so results in more net disposable income and wealth for us. Buying washers and dryers to cut down on dry cleaning bills and to avoid laundromats are generally worth the loan, especially if carefully shop for sales and financing. Similarly, if we have a family, buying a freezer to allow us to buy what we will consume over a season in bulk and on sale. Borrowing for a car makes sense under several, but not all, situations. In addition to dealerships, credit unions often offer low interest loans on cars. For instance, borrowing for a newer, more reliable car may cost less than incurring large, fairly regular repairs on an older car and missing work. With the changing safety and connectivity technology that rapidly becomes suboptimal if not obsolete, it may more sense to lease a car than to buy one. However, we should be borrowing for safety and dependability, not luxuries at this stage, even if by doing so, we do make our neighbors jealous.

Positioning the car note within the framework of our asset and debt portfolio, we may be better off making a small down payment and financing the car at a lower interest rate when we're already borrowing with credit cards and other higher-priced debt. It makes sense to keep a car note when we're still establishing savings on the side for other emergencies that we would charge if we didn't have liquid cash. Then, if there is another emergency as there always seems to eventually be, we can cover it from our savings rather than having to borrow at higher credit card interest rates to cover that emergency. And we can pay off notes like these early when we can comfortably do so. Because car and house notes are secured by the car and house themselves however, if we ever do a miss a payment, they can be repossessed. Other, unsecured charges like last week's groceries and last month's vacation are much more difficult to repossess. So, it is important to pay the secured bills first if our fortunes reverse.

Borrowing for a house also makes sense where we think our income is stable, we intend to stay in that house for several years and the neighborhood housing market is fairly stable. However, owning a house is often more work with lawns to mow and repairs to cover, and there are a lot of indirect expenses of owning a home. So, our lifestyle should be able to accommodate those extra responsibilities, and our monthly payment should be small enough that we have some slack in our budget to buy lawnmowers and repair plumbing and periodically paint houses as needed. While our house payment may be largely the same as if we were renting, we are building equity in the home, so when we're ready to sell, we might receive money back after paying the balance of the mortgage. Fixed mortgage rates, while often more expensive than variable interest rates, provides us with certainty that we will likely be able to continue to afford the mortgage payments. We will be asked whether we want a 15-year mortgage or a 30-year mortgage. Over the long-term, the 15-year mortgage is usually much less expensive, but at the cost of a higher monthly payments, which if we have credit card balances may mean that we pay them off slower, more than offsetting what we save in the shorter house payment.

We can leverage wanting a shorter term and/or a more certain interest rate by implementing an easy finance strategy. We can pay a little more than is required with every house payment. In the case of a variable rate mortgage, we hedge the uncertainty in interest rates by making the minimum house payment that would be required if it were a fixed interest mortgage payment. The extra that we pay reduces the principal balance that we owe. If in future years the interest rate goes up, they will go up on a much smaller balance so that essentially the differences between the two rates even out over time. Normally, this strategy actually results in our paying off our house sooner, and even if our minimum payment eventually does exceed the payment that we would have had at fixed rates, we can see that trend coming far in advance and may be making more income to cover the higher payment. Another strategy is to ask the lender to calculate the payment for both the 15-year and the 30-year terms, then, take out the 30-year note in case we might need to cut some spending in the future, but pay the 15-year rate for as long as we can stand. For both of these strategies, the sooner we start, the more interest expense we save and the wealthier we are, although it's hard to see that on a monthly basis because our progress seems to happen so slowly. A variation on these strategies is to make another, smaller payment in the middle of each month. That sometimes works very well for those of us who are paid twice a month or every other week. Even small amounts like $20/month add up to reduce the amount we owe, allowing us to pay off our houses much earlier than indicated on the original loan term.

Regardless of the type of borrowing, we generally shouldn't be borrowing for longer periods than what we're *borrowing for* lasts. That is, if we're using credit cards to charge dinner and a movie, we should pay off at least that amount when the credit card bill comes due. In months where we haven't bought an asset, we should be looking to paying both the amount of purchases listed at the top of the statement, and the amount of interest, plus a bit more to pay off the balances on past long-term purchases. Some of us, dubbed "transactors," are very cautious with credit cards, paying the balance in full every month so as to get the free cash back and avoid all interest expense. Some of us then use debit cards for most purchases to avoid going into debt. Most of us are "revolvers" who carry credit card debt from month to month and paying interest on our average daily balance.[176] Per NerdWallet's calculations, that results in about $904 in interest expense per year for the revolvers.[177]

What Expenses Do We Normally Charge?

Where we choose to use credit cards, we also admit that we charge unnecessary expenses, which is an opportunity for us to cut back spending if we want. Where we choose to use charge cards, we are paying over $900 in credit card interest each year, on over $15,000 in credit card debt balances.[178]

We put a lot of our medical expenses on credit cards, especially when they are unexpected.[179] NerdWallet explains, the average annual out-of-pocket medical spending per person was $1,054 in 2015. If all of this were charged and only minimum payments were made each month, it would cost $471 in interest and take 70 months to pay off.[180] Of course, by then nearly 6 more years would have passed, and we'd owe medical expenses for those years, too.

Our Bill Payments Interact

When we can afford to, it is usually most rational for us to pay off credit card debt first, because this debt normally bears the highest interest rate. We may even consider consolidating credit card debt, especially where we can get no balance transfer fees and an attractive, limited time low interest rate. However, most of us that are revolvers and who pay off our credit cards succumb to temptation and begin running up balances again, whereas if we had made a payment on our house, that debt would probably be paid down for good. So, such advice is only good advice if we know that we normally have the self-discipline to avoid charging expenses in the future. Similarly, home ownership builds savings in a tangible, useful asset whereas renting does not. Even so,

NerdWallet found that renters pay almost 50% less credit card interest than their home-owning friends.[181]

Stealth Debts

We might also have stealth debts that are not evident, but rather are contingent on our own or our family's actions. For example, we might have cosigned for our children's student loans. If our children do not get good jobs or handle their finances correctly, we are responsible for that debt in full. That could affect our ability to retire, and in some cases, past due student loans will be paid by diverting our yearly tax refunds from us to the lender. Or, we may have overdraft protection on our checking account. While that protects our credit score and prevents late fees when we make a mistake in our account, it has fees of its own that we don't usually budget for.

On the flip side, we also have a stealth asset in the form of cash back bonuses that accrue on our credit cards. These bonuses act as a kind of small income stream in themselves, and if managed well, can add up to quite a bit over time. Banks have different reward systems though, and some rewards expire, essentially giving the money we've earned right back to the bank, in return for nothing. Some financial advisers suggest that the cash balance can be used to pay off debt. Others save it for irregular expenses, like vacations, and still others save it for economic shocks. If we know that our credit card just seems to creep up no matter what we do, it makes sense to use this for the irregular expenses from economic shocks. That is, for many of us, it makes sense to use the cash back as a kind of short-term savings account, even though it earns no interest in its own right.

Small Businesses

Our business income is still often irregular, and because of seasonality and economic trends, may always be. This calls for crafty budgeting on our part. When times are good, we must be careful not to assume they will always be, and automatically set aside a cushion for leaner times. At the same time, the success may be real and permanent, and we'd hate to miss an opportunity to grow our business to bigger levels. This calls for wisdom. We can check with several financial professionals, and if we have been doing the books ourselves, it's time to hire a CPA. We need a strong team around us. This should include a CPA that we can trust for general advice as well as specific tax advice, a good relationship with the staff at our bank, other financial advisers like a trusted insurance agent, and attorney for questions as they arise and help in our own personal business, like the drafting of wills and trusts. Because businesses vary so widely by industry, it's hard to know what to do without a strong financial team that can work together with one another, and team members will often contradict in their advice. It's important to remember that advice involves judgment, so to some extent, all our team members are guessing. Even so, thoughtful, educated guesses stand a better chance of success than our gut feeling alone.

We also must watch our expenses. We use our businesses to support local causes in our community through contributions in kind like technical help and merchandise. We sponsor local amateur sports teams.[182] Taxes become an increasingly bigger factor. Taxes are complex. They're not just income taxes, but also multi-state sales taxes and because we are hiring employees, we will also have employment taxes and worker compensation laws to abide by. We may offer our employees benefits to reward their loyalty and avoid the cost of having to replace them when they can get jobs elsewhere. We may even encounter a tax audit. The added level of complexity makes it worth our while to hire more financial professionals. Certified Public Accountants (CPAs) are one set of vetted professionals, and they can represent us if we find ourselves under a tax audit. However, we need to declare all our income and pay attention to some of the expenses that are more sensitive to income tax audits. These expenses include: charitable write-offs, business meals, claiming 100% business use of the vehicle that we drive, large write-offs of activities that could be construed as hobbies, and writing off day-trading losses on our business books. Rental losses are also more susceptible to audit. Foreign operations are sometimes common in our businesses and they pose an additional tax risk. While the amount of income tax is not at risk, failing to disclose foreign bank accounts can result in large penalties imposed by the Internal Revenue Service (IRS).

Our spending has gone up because we have a successful business to run. Often, we finance these expenses. We have more credit card debt, which in turn leads to more interest expense than our employee-friends. NerdWallet found that households led by self-employed people pay about 40% more in credit card interest than those who work for someone else.[183] However, credit card interest rates might be higher than other sources of financing we can get now that we are rising up through the socioeconomic ladder.

As mentioned earlier, the Small Business Administration (SBA) makes loans to businesses such as ours and provides useful information on managing debts. It might also help us to set up a line of credit with our bank. The line of credit may be more useful to us than a normal loan because we pay no interest until we actually borrow against the pre-approved credit limit. The interest rates on both SBA loans and lines of credit tend to be much less than credit card interest rates, allowing us to financially inch further forward.

While we don't feel that we have much income to spare, our business does support us, and it's worth looking at how we can protect both the business and our personal wealth. Our personal wealth is exposed when we operate as a single owner, unincorporated "sole proprietorship" or in a general partnership. In both a sole proprietorship and a basic general partnership, there is no separation of ownership and management. Owners are jointly and severally liable for all the debts of a partnership, meaning that one partner can bind the partnership, and all other partners must personally make good on that promise if the partnership itself does not. This liability feature makes general partnerships very undesirable.

Partnerships can take the form of limited partnerships. Even though a partnership is a limited partnership, there must be at least one general partner who is in charge of the management of the company and is liable for all partnership obligations. Those who are limited partners have no say in management, but their personal assets are protected so that they cannot lose more on this investment than the amount of their investment that is kept within the partnership.

The most common business entity in the U.S. is the corporation.[184] Our investment in the company is translated into corporate ownership shares, and our risk of loss is generally limited to our investment, which is crucial should we want to build our own personal wealth. Had we remained a sole proprietorship or a general partner in a partnership, we would remain personally liable for all the debts of the business, including the company debts that our partners authorized but of which we did not approve. Ownership shares may be voting or nonvoting, and we can issue multiple classes of stock, including classes of stock that do not vote. Corporations are governed by their board of directors, who are elected by the owners of the company. The board appoints officer/employees of the company to operate the day-to-day operations of the business. Corporate finances are separate from that of the owners. To incorporate, we need approval from the state in which we want to incorporate. This is normally an easy, streamlined process from the state's perspective, but there may be legal implications that emerge if we do not seek legal advice on incorporation early in the process. There are legal and tax implications to the way in which we operate this company.

One tax implication of a corporation is whether we elect to have our company taxed as a regular corporation, or as an "S" corporation. In a regular corporation, the corporation is taxed on its income annually, and to the extent that the corporation pays out its earnings to shareholders as dividends, the shareholders receiving those dividends are taxed again on the dividends that they receive, although usually at a preferable, lower tax rate. Still, the dividends are subject to two layers of tax, and for many of us, that's at least one too many layers of tax. S corporations are not directly taxed. Instead, we owners of an S corporation are taxed on our respective shares of the corporation income at our personal income tax rates. Distributions from the S corporation are not taxed, resulting in a single level of tax. Our personal income tax rates may be higher than the corporate rate though. And, there are other S Corporation restrictions that make this form of business inflexible. Noncash property distributions are generally taxed, and taxable profits and losses are passed on to owners strictly according to their ownership percentage. Only U.S. citizens or residents may be shareholders in an S corporation and the total number of shareholders must be 100 or less, where a shareholder is loosely defined as a taxpayer, making two spouses one owner if they file their tax return jointly. All owners must consent to the S corporation status for it to be approved.

And, while incorporation is popular, another entity such as a Legal Liability Company, or LLC, may be a better fit for our company. The LLC offers the limited liability feature of corporations, and the company can elect to be taxed as a partnership, which is similar in many ways to how an S corporation is taxed. There are no restrictions on non-U.S. citizens and non-resident owners, nor is the number of shareholders limited to 100. There is no requirement for a board of directors or officers, as with a corporation. As with corporations, an LLC or partnership should have a distinctly separate financial books and records.

"There's Got to Be Something Better Than in the Middle"[185]

We need to juggle several financial balls at once. We need to increase our income, through returns on assets and higher wages or business income. We need to reduce our long-term expenses, sometimes spending more currently. This means that we need to shop for bargains constantly, especially on more expensive items. We need to avoid buying toys and other material goods that amuse us—but only momentarily. Where we can reduce expenses, reduce. Where we can purge expenses, purge. Where we can delay expenses, delay.

For example, we need to periodically review our mortgage: does it pay for us to refinance? Do we owe less than 80% of what our home is worth, which could mean that if asked, our lender would stop charging monthly Private Mortgage Insurance (PMI), reducing our monthly payment and allowing us to save the difference? Can we delay expenses like replacing cars until it makes financial sense to do so?

We need a new sophistication in balancing our assets and debt. In particular, we need new asset and debt skills altogether. And, we need the habits and self-discipline to use those skills consistently.

If We Know What is Needed, Why Don't We Do It?

Because it is contrary to what we learned and believe to have worked when we were poorer, and because if we had done some of these things when were poorer, we fear we would have been worse off. Those fears may be justified, at least in part.

We may also be emotionally frustrated with money, with tv, luxury in our face, and our own wages stagnating. We just don't see the progress that we were promised throughout our childhood that if we just worked hard enough, we would get ahead. Employers are demanding more work from all of us just to keep our jobs. This pushes us all in huddled masses against our natural, physical work limits, meaning hardly anyone "gets ahead." We could make the effort to change or work harder, but would it matter?

We see our friends with a lifestyle that we want now, and partly out of a sense of wanting to belong and be respected, we want those items to and use credit to get them. That is, we don't dissociate our value as a person from the amount of wealth that we have, and the amount of wealth that others can see. Partly out of a lifestyle that is just too busy and sometimes leaves us exhausted, we make more expensive convenience purchases and charge them, thinking that we will figure out how to pay for them once we have time to take a breath. We can't clearly see when we will have time to take a breath, and we fear what would happen if we were to pass away before our children are raised.

Even so, we fear taking on debt, having seen so many of us in our lives mismanage debt. We fear being unable to pay debt. We fear never getting out of debt, and that interest charges will make us poorer still and perhaps unable to retire. These fears are legitimate. Researchers found that when relieved of all their debt, an experimental group of vendors were in as much debt as those who received no debt relief within a year, largely due to economic shocks.[186] To avoid being in this situation requires *so much* abundance that, even after overspending or procrastinating, there's still enough slack to manage most shocks.[187]

How Much, If at All, Should We Change Those Assumptions?

Financial shocks are *emotionally* frustrating. They knock us off our budgeted path, which makes some of us want to quit in futility and go back to our old habits. Our brain is still hard wired to the old habits. Fortunately, it's now also wired to our new habits, so we're not having to relearn new habits, just resume them, and that's an easier task then when we were just getting started.

When faced with financial shocks, some of us just want to feel better, and buying something fun or pretty helps us do that. When that sounds like us, saving a little beyond what we think we need for shocks to include a little something for ourselves during these times can help. We get the palliative benefit that takes some pressure off without the harm of going in debt because we've prepared for needing that extra, emotional boost. And, by having set a target limit for that spending, we've not overindulged which would put us on a worse path still.

That is, we need to tend to our very real emotions about money and spending, but still honor the rational parts of our brain. We need to honor the rational side, for example, when we combat our tendency for conspicuous consumption of both goods and experiences. We need to honor the rational side when we combat our fear of debt. Sometimes, debt pays off for us in the long run. The length of time over which we evaluate decisions continues to lengthen. The wealthier we get, the less we stop looking at immediate needs and the best decision for today, and the more we look toward getting through this month, and later, through this year and this lifetime and beyond.

How Might We Best Help Those in Need?

We are best helped when other acknowledge us and our struggle. In public discourse, the wealthy are skilled at getting attention for their causes, and some of the situations of our poorer friends make much more dramatic news. We acknowledge that those who are poorer are in greater need, but that doesn't mean that we aren't in need. We need lower taxes than the rich to continue to support our families and ignore inevitable economic shocks.

Advocating for higher wages also helps because while there is truth to the argument that if wages rise, prices will rise, wages are only a portion of the sales price of products. The cost of goods, other expenses like utilities and profits are also part of the price and they do not go up proportionately to rises in wages. So, if wages go up 10%, prices will go up, but by less than 10%, leaving us with extra money to make strategic purchases, pay off debt or invest.

Government support to help finance affordable skill sets, whether in the form of supporting higher education or affordable student loans are also very helpful in giving us the help we need to increase our income. After all, we don't mind working for our money, but we would like the chance to advance and prosper.

CHAPTER 7

Moving from Upper-Middle to Lower-Upper Class: The First Stage of "Rich"

"Movin' on up to the East Side....We finally got a piece of the pie."[88]

Wₑ're finally getting to be financially comfortable. However, we're not ready to stop climbing yet.

Life at this Level: Did Someone Say "(Pre-owned) Lexis?"

We are generally safer in day-to-day life than we were when we were poorer. We have more control of nearly everything that affects our lives. We have more mobility and will move for a better career opportunity, or in the alternative, pick up a second residence.

We try to buy better, tastier, and healthier food, perhaps shopping at farmers' markets and for organics. We are more educated and more likely to have at least a 4-year college degree. We use that education daily in broad ways; we try to make more educated consumer choices in homes, clothing, and cars. We are concerned about how our purchases affect not only ourselves but our community, the environment, and the world. Philanthropy becomes more than a way to improve the world because it's fun and profitable. Philanthropy becomes a social activity, tax write-off and way to network for both business and social purposes. We have no more leisure time, but we may have more choice in how we spend the time that we have and can afford to have housekeeping and other tasks outsourced.

We are not happier than when we were poorer, though,[189] nor are we less stressed. However, our sources of stress have changed from keeping everything running without or through economic shocks to positioning our lives for excellence. Life is actually very competitive for us if we are one of the first in our family to reach this level because the money is there to live this lifestyle, but the connections are not.[190] This means that we must win on merit alone. Merit takes our personal attention and time, so time is more important than small amounts of money and clipping coupons, although we still shop for sales on bigger ticket items. Details are critical to success. For example, a court ruling on a legal document could turn on the placement of a comma.

Our family structures are more stable, and we have more resources with which to deal with instabilities as they arise. Our parenting focuses on getting our children access to appropriate connections, schooling, and excellent coaching for their extracurricular activities, so that we raise well-rounded, educated children who are poised to recognize their full potential.

Our friends are generally wealthier as well, and we are more likely to discuss ideas than sports. These ideas inspire us and can be quite helpful in investment and business. We are less likely to give money to relatives who are not working, and less likely to allow them to move in with us. Our personal and emotional concerns are increasingly more likely to be shared with paid, degreed professionals, not friends and families. We begin to carefully consider our public image, and violations of our privacy are taken very seriously.

It depends on where we live, but on average, we have household income between about $75,000 to just over $120,000, nationally.[191] Most of us have relatively secure jobs with benefits and the ability to save. Most of us have a four-year college degree, and many of us have advanced degrees. If we live outside of expensive cities, we're generally homeowners, with the median price of our home at just over $200,000.[192] We drive newer cars that are generally still under warranty. We may have high quality, numbered artwork. We are more protective of our material possessions, separately insuring those that are most special to us. We aspire to break out of the middle class; even so, we still very strongly identify with being middle class.[193]

With this income, we buy the groceries that we want first, then maximize the unit cost for the items we've chosen rather than looking for the cheapest alternative with little regard for quality. We pay off our bills monthly without sacrificing our long-term goals. But, this takes active financial management on our part.

Income and Expenses

We have more high-paying job opportunities than we had before. We have the opportunity to change jobs and negotiate a salary increase, and we also have opportunities to invest and cut expenses, so the time to manage our finances increases and we should be assessing not only whether the opportunity is worthwhile, but whether the opportunity is worthwhile to us given the other opportunities we miss in pursuing one opportunity over the others. That is, there is an "opportunity cost" which is equal to the potential benefit lost by taking one opportunity when another opportunity is available. For example, if we take a year off to pursue a higher education degree, the forgone wages are the opportunity cost, which is part of the total cost of that education. With a limited amount of time and at this economic stage, the answer isn't cutting more coupons, so much as raising our income level and returns on investment, doing some tax planning, and at least semi-annually auditing our bills to cancel low-value services with recurring charges.

To handle our more complex financial situation, many of us use something called "mental accounting."[194] Richard Thaler is credited with naming this term, but his large body of work basically explains how many of this handle the complexity of our financial lives, finding that we have different mental "buckets" of money that we match to our various financial goals. Mental accounting is often less formal than a detailed budget and both can be used simultaneously. For example, we have pension money, which in our mind is in a very different bucket than pizza money, which is likely in a different budget than vacation money. When deciding where to go on vacation, we benchmark our vacation spending to the vacation budget, not to all the money we have in the world. The different buckets are not only for different purposes in our minds, they have different priorities for whether we contribute to them and what we withdraw. Only in extreme cases would we withdraw from our retirement funds, for example, but we might spend vacation money yearly and regular operating money whenever needed. If we can save and invest safely in appropriate buckets and avoid costly expenses like divorces and penalties from failing to disclose foreign bank accounts, we are well on our way to building assets and protecting them. And, there are some costly expenses for which we can insure to protect our overall wealth.

At this stage, we should have good health care coverage, because an extensive injury or chronic illness can wipe away our savings if we are uninsured. We might want income replacement insurance if we do not have a strong nest egg. We have robust liability insurance for our home(s). Liability insurance is a contract where the insurer agrees to pay for unintentional damages that we cause to other people and property. We check our insurance for exemptions, like dog bites. We are best protected when we have property insurance on our own car (including uninsured motorist coverage) and home to the extent that we cannot afford to replace it. Property insurance protects our financial interest in physical property when its damaged by other people, accidents, and natural disasters. The most prepared of us have long-term care (nursing home) insurance, which is much cheaper if bought while we are younger than if bought right before we need it. At our best, we have enough life insurance to bury us, pay our debts, and ensure that our children are provided for until they graduate at whatever level of schooling that we think is appropriate for them. And, we consider an umbrella policy for millions of dollars for other, miscellaneous liabilities that might arise. In short, we now have assets worth protecting, and insurance is often the best, most affordable way to protect them.

Assets and Liabilities

Being on the upper side of the wealth divide, our wealth has been growing over the last few years. That growth has been outpacing any growth found in lower socioeconomic levels, where income growth has generally been flat or down slightly.[195] The divide between rich and poor has been growing, and we have been benefactors of this divide. Our real wealth has also increased, as shown in the chart on the below.

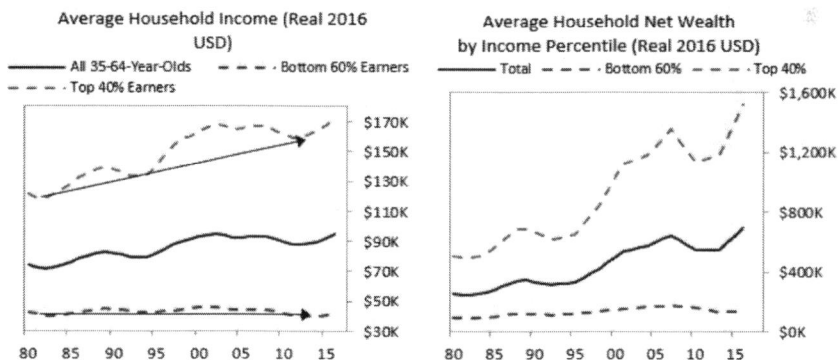

Source: https://www.linkedin.com/pulse/our-biggest-economic-social-political-issue-two-economies-ray-dalio/

We are concerned about growing our wealth and we don't just want to protect it for us, we want to pass it down to our heirs.[196]

Our increase in wealth comes largely from having our hard-saved money in the form of stocks and other financial investments. Our portfolios are shifting: a lesser percentage may be in our house, life insurance or retirement, and we hold more investments in liquid stocks and bonds that can be cashed in if needed. However, there are still almost half of us that have less than $1,000 in savings accounts.[197]

How does this happen? We often have a house, but it's highly mortgaged. We often have retirement funds of some kind, but they're often tied up and we can't reach them. And, for many of us, if our employer did not make saving for retirement mandatory, we opted not to save for retirement yet, thinking that retirement is far off in the future whereas other more urgent needs are not. We may have cash value in life insurance, but uncertain investment returns and sales commissions have offset a lot of the investment over the cost of term life insurance, especially in the early years. We may have some investments in short-term savings accounts and investment portfolios, but we also have car notes, perhaps student debt, and credit card debt that offsets the traction that these investments might give us in moving up.

Those of us who are rising are in the habit of thinking for a longer term than when we were poor and planning, and it's paying off. Academic studies tout the benefits of planning. For example, one researcher found[198] that when people had more time to anticipate incoming money, they saved more of it. The permanence of payments may also be a factor in how much we choose to save. Parker[199] studied tax cuts, finding that a temporary, end-of-year reduction in Social Security tax for high-income wage earners was spent when received rather than averaged evenly over the fiscal year.

Our college accounts should be funded, but often are not. According to Fidelity Investments, we should have at least $2,000 times the age of each of our children in our college fund. If we stay on track with this amount we should have roughly half the cost of attending a public, in-state university.[200]

But what about the other half? This is frequently borrowed. Over recent years, student loan balances have jumped tremendously.[201] We approach higher education costs by shopping for the best deal for our particular student, which is often not the lowest cost college. We use our savings. We cut back on living expenses to pay what we can as we go. We seek out scholarships from athletics, merit, and general welfare funds. We take out loans, government loans first, with subsidized interest,[202] avoiding parental cosigning where possible. We protect our retirement and hope to leave some of it to our children.

To pass this wealth down, we consider writing a will and when operating at our best, we definitely do so if we are responsible for supporting minor or incapacitated family members. At a minimum, we periodically check that we have designated a beneficiary on our investment accounts so that those accounts will be distributed upon our death in accordance with our wishes.

Business Owners

Special financial planning skills are needed for business owners. The business itself may be quite valuable on the open market because of its tangible assets like machinery and equipment and intangible assets like customer lists. However, the value of a small business dissipates very quickly if the key person or people cannot work due to injury, illness, or death. In a family business when the key person is a family member, the emotional strain means that other family members are understandably less productive when one member of the family falls victim to a tragedy. While less productivity is understandable, it hurts the value of the business sharply and quickly. We prepare succession plans, so that our businesses, especially those that rest on the expertise of key people, can be sold quickly if necessary, preserving most of their value which would otherwise decline at an alarming rate.[203]

To protect the normal income stream from our businesses, we shop for and purchase business interruption insurance, which replaces the income from our businesses when casualties prevent us from operating them. Auto liability insurance covers employees on company business, and sometimes accidents involving permissive operators, which are drivers authorized by the company, when driving for non-business purposes. We have purchased employer's non-owned auto coverage for when our employees conduct even brief errands in their own cars because sometimes personal auto insurance coverage will refuse to cover such accidents. General business insurance covers liability from accidents that happen within the scope of the business, except for intentional acts of employees, acts while intoxicated, discrimination, contractual obligations, and acts of officers and board members. We purchase separate insurance to cover the acts of officers and board members. We may elect specialty coverage for discrimination and sexual harassment. We purchase malpractice insurance that covers our work except for gross negligence, punitive damages, acts of uninsured subordinate employees, and defective products if we are professionals. By being adequately insured, we increase the chance of financially surviving a setback, because in part, it is tempting for attorneys, who work on a percent of the settlement, to settle for the insurance proceeds rather than to risk a protracted lawsuit with an uncertain judgment and the uncertain ability to collect.

Our succession plans may involve buyouts by people either within or from without the firm. We may put the company up for sale or seek a strategic merger with another firm. Alternatively, we may train replacements for key personnel, which should generally happen in advance.[204] However, identified successors can become impatient and conflicted. They want the challenges of greater leadership, but without our actual death. So, we sometimes write a mandatory retirement age into such agreements, as well as transition rules for our exit. For example, we may give extended, one- to two-year notice to the firm of our departure. Our children, who we have trained to be quite talented, especially do not want to wait or wish for our death, so if they have an interest in our firm, they will often leave a family business to pursue their own robust careers or entrepreneurial interests in their 40s if there is not a clear, near-term succession path. Even addressing the issue of retirement is difficult. Could we be that old? Could someone else really replace us successfully? Keeping our eye on wealth preservation is essential in this emotional process.

Other protection against liabilities is also essential. One bad lawsuit can put our business at risk, and our personal family wealth, too, if our businesses are not properly structured. So, we begin to establish employee handbooks and training, and other policy manuals. We have consulted with attorneys to make sure that we have chosen a business entity structure that limits our liability. We have consulted with accountants to limit the amount of assets at risk, including whether we are complying with tax filings and payments, which becomes increasingly complicated as we take on more employees. We have consulted with insurance professionals to minimize worker compensation liabilities and general business risks. And, our financial team routinely coordinates with one another to protect our interests. However, we don't just want to protect our business, we want to grow our business.

As we draw out wealth from the company and into our personal accounts, we tend to invest it in what states call "exempt assets." These are assets that are without any special legal protective structure but still protect us from creditors, who cannot take the assets, were we to go into personal bankruptcy. Depending on the state in which we live, protected assets could include: our family residence,[205] family farm, tools of the trade, one auto or other mode of transportation, life insurance, annuities and retirement accounts. However, most of these assets are not liquid, so we need some liquid cash, or access to liquidity in the form of a line of credit for paying living expenses, legal defense fees as they arise, and cash to cover economic shocks.

As the asset balances are shifting for the best of us, we begin to build wealth in long-term assets, we begin to protect short-term assets from creditors and possible bankruptcy.

One Person's Story

Buying a new cell phone—how a routine transaction in a day in the life sheds light on how successful people think.

I'm driving up in an 11½ year-old car with failing clearcoat. I will have the clear coat redone, but today is not that day. I have another, newer car if I need one, but very little time to attend to this detail. The steering wheel needs to be recovered because the leather is worn through to the padding. I bought this car new, and except for the clear coat, maintained it well. It has over 281,000 miles on it, but it still runs well. It's something of a curiosity to me—can I drive this car for 300,000 miles?

> **Lesson 1:** Looks can be deceptive. Not all successful people flash their wealth. See "The Millionaire Next Door."

> **Lesson 2:** Successful people are often busy people. They're good at tending to important financial decisions, but even they get frayed around the edges with some decisions. Money may be measured in dollars per hour or dollars per effort, not just total dollars.

> **Lesson 3:** Successful people often have spares of necessities or access to spares. Were I more successful, I'd probably spring for a concierge to take the car in for me.

> **Lesson 4:** Successful people appreciate quality. How they interpret that word varies, but the principal is fairly universal.

I go in to the cell phone store wanting to trade a Samsung Galaxy III, which is several years old but still in good shape, for the newest model, a water-resistant Galaxy 7. I am upgrading specifically to get cell phone service in the UK where I am traveling the next day. I know the phone and the alterations to my monthly plan that I want.

Lesson 5: Successful people not only plan ahead, they research ahead, keeping their eyes open for what they think that they might want or need, often several years in the future. This allows them to save either time or money, or both.

There are three cell phone plans advertised. The first comes with a 2-year contract—but is $50 cheaper in total than the other monthly plan. That plan is too binding for a family situation that is in flux, because by combining plans over the next year or so, we may be able to save more than $50, but there's another lesson here.

Lesson 6: Successful people routinely, automatically, have a longer time horizon than most. They don't feel like it's a struggle to "just get by." Looking at the scientific research, there are some very good reasons why thinking ahead is easier for wealthier people than for the poor, and the results prove out that successful people tend to use their advantage in this respect.

The second plan is a bit more per month and comes with an installment contract. The third plan is to pay for the phone up front. I compare the last two plans. As I am doing the math on my phone, the sales person explains that the monthly payment plan has a 0% interest rate. I joke that the installment plan is 17 cents more expensive over the 2-year installment period. The salesman reiterates the cheapest monthly rate, and looks at me questioningly—can I afford the new model, or should we be looking at the previous model? I am amused that he seems to have not learned Lesson 1: Successful people generally do not flash their full wealth. I did show a spark of surprise at the sticker price, because as the newest Samsung model, it was still markedly cheaper and had the same functionality as the iPhone that I bought for my friend on his birthday last year. The salesman had no way to know that, and whether it's my car or my phone, I have no interest in whether the salesman thinks I have money or not, or whether he judges me by my possessions.

I normally prefer to buy things outright, but at a 0% interest, I almost have to buy this on the installment plan on the principal that one does not pass up a 0% loan. As one close to me once said, "at 0% interest, I'd finance gum."

I waiver, and the salesman explains that I can't buy it outright here—I have to use one of the two installment methods, but I can pay it off in a month if I'd like. That's a decision for another day. Living in a small beach town, the time that I would lose buying the phone elsewhere is not worth asserting my preference, and only some big box stores will set the phone up for me which I know that they will do for me here. In my mind, I am buying a bundled good—the phone, plus the set-up service. I can give a little.

> **Lesson 7:** Successful people buy a lot of convenience goods, especially if they save time. The more one makes per hour, the greater the opportunity cost[206] of wasting time on these things. (We see this in Los Angeles, for example, where sometimes people pay others to stand in line for them.)

I get the installment agreement and read it as the salesman sets up the phone. The agreement has a forced arbitration clause, which I object to on principal. Last August, I bought a car outright after rejecting that clause in the installment agreement. (I am not alone, see the activities outlined in various editions of "Consumer Reports," a fine magazine from the not-for-profit organization that has also objected to these clauses.) Here, as with the auto contract, I read the clause carefully, strike through the objectionable language and initial. I believe that I can make alterations before the contract is signed by both parties because the contract is really an offer until it's signed, and what I have done, in essence, is counter-offer. Before the seller signs the contract, the seller is free to object and not make the sale. I sign the last page and request a copy, which I get. The salesman assembles and staples the contract, counting the pages, but not noticing nor objecting to the changes in one of the middle pages. I get my phone, but with better contract terms. (The business law classes

I took in college have been some of the most valuable I have ever had, and my college internship as a consumer advocate was also invaluable.)

Lesson 8: Successful people often have higher education levels—they have more education, they value education, and they use their education.

So, How Do We Get More?

We have risen so far, largely through our own hard work and independent initiative. One thing that we need is just time: time to invest in our businesses and our lives, and time for the investments we've already made to grow.

Businesses reach a certain size where we can't do it all ourselves. Increasingly, financial, social, and political connections replace our individual production of a product or service as a central key to success.[207] We need access to key people, ideas, and venues. To connect, we must have an individual already approved by that group make the introductions.[208]

To meet these people and make connections, it helps us to spend our money on trend, or a little ahead of trend. We will be asked to contribute to charities, often organized by friends, colleagues, and other business associates. We may also need other people's money, and so banking relationships become important, as is our getting over our fear of being in debt. And, we need to insulate our assets to protect our families in case fortunes reverse by choosing our investments methodically.

Why Don't We Get More?

In trying to reach out to those in different social circles, often, we don't know where to begin. We are afraid to fail. We are afraid of debt. Fear of debt and fear of spending money to make money are likely based on the negative consequences that we or those close to us endured when we failed or took on debt.

Those fears are justified. But, we can mitigate the negative consequences of failure and debt in ways that we could not when we were poorer.

How Much, If at All, Should We Change Those Assumptions?

To some extent, increasing our social circle is organic to where we live, worship, and send our children to school. There are also professional organizations with which we can make connections and serve our profession. If we have a hobby about which we are passionate, we can meet through connecting with others who have the same hobby. Social media sites like LinkedIn also help build our social network.

Addressing how we reframe debt is a challenge, because we must question long held beliefs about debt. If we have our own business that is structured as a corporation or Limited Liability Company, we have protection from company creditors for liabilities. While we might lose our investment in the company, we won't lose our personal assets, except to the extent that we have cosigned for company debt or failed to pay employment taxes withheld from our employees' checks. It may go against our current thinking, but if the company cannot pay its debts, the company goes bankrupt, but we don't personally go bankrupt. Understanding that the consequences of failure are often much less than when we were poorer reframes the "should we borrow" conversation. Borrowing not only has fewer negative consequences, it can have more positive consequences.

Working with our CPAs and bankers, we can work to determine whether we are paying the least amount of expenses on our money borrowed. This normally means paying the lowest interest rate, but also includes costs of debt balance transfers and fees to refinance. Some debt consolidation or refinancing might be advisable. Working with that same team, we can determine what percent of return we currently earn on our assets and look to borrow money at an interest rate below that return on assets percentage, especially in the case where we own our own business. Using that money to grow the business allows us to expand at a reasonable risk, without risking our personal assets. We act on our knowledge to protect our family financially where the company does make money by drawing off a reasonable salary to build our wealth personally. That way, if the company were to go bankrupt, we would have a savings cushion to support our family and start another business or line of work. While we don't want to see creditors hurt, we understand that they are putting their interests first, and we put our family's interest first as well.

How Might We Best Help Others from Here?

While we have talked about controlling spending and keeping expenses lower, as upper middle class transcending to lower upper class, we do have the luxury, and some would argue the responsibility to give back to our community. Contributing money and time to charities may result in reciprocal financial benefits, but more importantly, it adds more purpose to our lives, which are no longer consumed with merely getting by. Contributing money directly, contributing goods, services and organizational expertise from our business, and contributing our time are ways to help the next person behind us reach their goals and dreams.

CHAPTER 8

How Much Are the Flight Upgrades? From Lower-Upper to Middle-Upper— Comfortably Rich

"Let's paint the picture of a perfect place—they've got it better than what anyone's told you."[209]

—————

Moving up to the upper class means to some that we have arrived! Ironically, we see those who make more money still, aspire to do the same, and we often don't feel rich. Yes, there's greed, but we fear falling out of our hard-earned gains. We still face short-term cash crunches, and some of the non-financial problems that we have seem to have followed us here. As hard as we're working, the most elite luxury goods still seem elusive as we meet people who are richer than ourselves, and the increased wealth in the upper socioeconomic levels push competition for those goods, which drives the prices on those goods higher. These characteristics are reflected in our politics, and we tend to be more conservative than our poorer brethren, or our richer brethren who feel confident that they have more than they can ever spend.

That does not mean that wealth has no benefits. There are fewer external threats to our well-being. We have a greater locus of control over our lives, and we solve nearly all the problems that having money can solve. We live longer and have healthier lives, both physically and mentally, than our poorer friends and family.[210] We have more access to higher-quality health care and many of us with ongoing health problems opt in to closed, private physician practices to ensure near on-demand continued access; but, we have still not found a way to cheat death entirely. We have less stressful, less polluted, less dangerous living and working environments. What stress we do have, we regularly offset with manicures, pedicures, facials, massages, vacations, travel, etc.

Life at this Level—Living the American Dream

We are better looking. We have more access to fashion and start leaning toward designer pieces or pieces made in very limited lots that distinguishes our style from the masses. We can afford and purchase good tailoring. We have more access to stylish haircuts, teeth straightening and whitening, Botox, fillers, and other physical enhancements that keep us looking young. We eat better, and are more likely to eat locally grown, carefully processed and prepared foods, which are better for us than Twinkies, which are cheaper. We are only momentarily hungry or thirsty. We have the house that we want and the car that we want.

We readily pay for time and know how much our time is worth. We pay for direct flights, airport lounges, to board airlines first and have ample overhead access. Our cell phones must have worldwide access. We pay to drive the faster lanes on the expressway. We pay valets to park and pick up our cars, and sometimes wash them while we lunch. We pay to have our houses cleaned, our yards and pools cared for, and to help with the care of our children. We have few reasons to be fearful, although if we are moving up in economic stature, we may inappropriately bring old fears with us without even realizing it. We have the money to afford legal counsel to defend ourselves and our rights against criminal charges and injustices. We may not have an attorney on retainer, but we have their number handy and know they will return our call. We win these court fights in disproportionate numbers compared to those of lesser income. We still worry about money, but the amount of money it takes to be worth worrying about goes up.[211]

But a new, more subtle threat arises. If we're moving up the economic ladder, we relate to those with less money, including the people who help us by cleaning houses and maintaining yards. It's easy to confuse our help with our friends because it was our friends and family who would have helped you with these things before. Other people who you've known want favors (money), and among our new acquaintances are those who will pose as friends just for the favors. Jimmy Buffet wrote a song, "Gypsies in the Palace," about those "friends." In some cases, we are the target of frauds, extortion, or threats of kidnapping. As such, many of us elect to keep a low public profile. We often live in gated communities or homes with solid privacy fences, but within the gates, the windows and doors have no bars. We have security systems that include multiple cameras. When we socialize, we tend to join private clubs that limit photography and guard our identities. The problem is worse if our personalities are introverted, because we're less likely to meet new people, especially since as we work our way up, there are fewer people to meet. There are even support groups that are limited to the wealthy and the problems that accompany that wealth. Of course, members of such groups also bring each other into our own deals. And, we train our children in how to protect their inheritances by sending them to financial life skills retreats. It's important to know when to talk about the required pre-nuptial or marital agreements in a relationship. Our wealth advantages are frequently not reflected in our children's psychological adjustment to life. More of our children are clinically depressed, and alcohol and drug use are higher than that for inner city kids.

Sometimes we send our children to tutors, not because they need it academically, but we want someone to watch our teenagers while we work, and a nanny seems condescending.

We are a growing group.[212] Our social and professional groups are broader. These groups are larger, more extensive, and more international. Nearly all of us have passports and have used them. It's not unusual to be invited to political inaugurations and parties in different cities, nationally and internationally. Our businesses are also international, and occasional international travel is commonplace, with most of us registered with international travel security services such as Global Access.

Commerce at this level moves us from being independent to interdependent on others of similar economic stature, or "networking." People we don't like are tolerated because of their desired connections to our commerce, comingling friendships and business associates and lending superficiality to our emotional ties to others in our group.

Contrary to popular belief though, we may move to better neighborhoods, but don't move to better cities.[213] We are geographically tied to our families and social networks, and can afford to (and do) travel or vacation to "better" cities at will, staying at better hotels with amenities such as lighted make up mirrors and happy hours on-site.[214] It's the middle class that is likely to move, being both able to move and occasionally travel to see old friends, but at the same time, finding frequent travel too costly. For the same reasons, family members are likely to join those who move shortly thereafter.

The opportunity to buy in bulk when it's advantageous to do so often exists and is done. , The pattern where costs decline per unit as more is purchased is called, "economies of scale." It is generally cheaper per hour to hire cleaning services for an entire day than for a couple of hours. This is because the cleaners themselves can avoid unbillable hours traveling from multiple jobs and focus on one. It generally also pays to buy pool supplies, cleaning supplies, and depletable household products like paper towels in bulk because it saves money per unit to do so, and generally at this income level, we live in residences that are large enough to store the extra products neatly and safely. We look for cash discounts for prepaying bills or paying an entire year at a time, as is typical with some insurance policies. When given two different payment options (e.g. "zero down" or interest-free), we do the math, comparing both options to paying cash, and choose the cheapest option, thus preserving our wealth and making us able to afford more goods and services still. That said, we can also afford to forego buying in bulk and pay the convenience package premiums when it suits us to do so. Delivery services like Amazon Prime are used.

Incentives like freebies, like event tickets, comped services, or products become increasingly common. That's somewhat ironic since we're in a better economic position to pay for products, and less likely to need them. The ability to be indifferent is what makes some sellers try harder to earn our business.

We still watch our own money very closely, but often employ trusted financial advisers to make appropriate investments in stocks, bonds, real estate, and smaller ventures. That is, we often dabble as venture capitalists.

Not everyone who appears to be at this level really is, though. People who are not as financially blessed will appear to be because of their access to credit. There is an entire line of "fake it 'til you make it" thinking where we try to impress others, who we ironically think aren't faking it too, so that, being in with the right crowd, we will get richer through better deals and connections. These wannabes, or poseurs abound, and they try to prove their worth through outspending our colleagues and neighbors. Only a few of us are, or want to be famous. Quite the contrary, we seek out private clubs and exclusive experiences to avoid interaction with and exposure to masses of people. Violating our privacy, for example dishing to the media, is not easily forgiven.

Arguably, we should be happier than when we were poorer, and we are, but not by all that much.[215] It's not the extra wealth per se that makes us happier, it's knowing that we are well off and have the extra control over our lives that wealth gives us that we like. Having money but not having control over our lives makes us less happy than say, someone in the upper middle class who is living beneath their means and has stability and control over their life. Some of us who receive sudden wealth, like a lottery jackpot, can experience more distrust and depression, even though we have more money.[216] Research on lottery winners show that while they feel good about winning, they are not significantly happier than non-winners and enjoy ordinary activities less than non-winners.[217] Those of us who have earned our wealth enjoy it more than those of us who have won the lottery or inherited it.

Income and Expenses

We often earn our money by being more entrepreneurial in our thoughts and actions, even when working for someone else's company. We might also be an exceptionally skilled or talented worker, such as an actor, professional athlete, or favored plastic surgeon. When we are in business for ourselves, we may be serial entrepreneurs, or parallel entrepreneurs. We are very busy, unlike the typical old school leisure class of 100 years ago. Where we have multiple business interests, we might have multiple liquidity events where we cash out multiple times in our lives as an entrepreneur or corporate executive. We've learned that this income structure can be much less costly to us with proper tax planning. We are also in the crosshairs of the IRS more often. The IRS' reach is international because they routinely exchange financial information with their tax treaty partners, and tax information exchange agreements with non-treaty partners. Their reach is particularly strong with other countries in the Mutual Collection Assistance Program.[218]

The ability to afford not only necessities but also luxury items has been discovered by governments worldwide. We have a new enemy—income taxes. Income taxes behave differently than most other costs. Generally, costs can be described as either fixed or variable, or perhaps as some combination of both. Fixed costs do not change based on our income. For example, if we lease a car, the amount of the lease payment does not change over the lease term. It especially does not change with our income level. Apartment rent is an example of a fixed cost. Fixed costs stay the same over a "relevant range," which is the income level at which we normally operate. Fixed costs contrast to variable costs which do rise directly with income. We don't see many strictly variable costs in the consumer economy, although many of our costs vary with usage instead of income. For example, if we drive more, we pay more for gas. Indirectly though, as our income rises, our standard of income tends to rise, pushing up the costs of food, clothing and entertainment. As such, these costs tend to behave like variable costs in that they go up with our standard of living, which in turn tends to go up with our income. In some cases, like in the case of many utilities, there is a base fee with an additional fee for usage. This would be part fixed and part variable, or a "mixed cost." Income taxes don't follow any of these patterns.

Income taxes work in a way that is almost opposite of economies of scale. Income tax rates are generally "progressive," meaning that the more we earn, the higher the tax rate becomes. At the lowest income levels, there is no tax, and in the United States, one might be able to receive "taxes" back when none were withheld due to the Earned Income Credit. Tax rates then start low but rise with income. First, the Earned Income Credit is completely phased out. Then tax filers become taxpayers. Then the amount of tax shifts upward on the higher levels of income only. So, someone at the high end of the lower class or the low end of the middle class likely receives an earned income credit if they have children, and that credit may not only wipe out their tax due but give them a refund on top of it. A typical taxpayer in this bracket making $15 per hour would make about $30,000 per year. In 2016 with four people in that household, about $22,000 would escape income tax, and the remaining $8,000 would be taxed at 10%, or $800 before earned income credit. They are subject to Social Security and Medicare taxes on their earnings, which was 7.65% of their wages in early 2017. For that hypothetical family making $15 per hour, that's about $2,295 in Social Security and Medicare tax.

People in the middle-middle class have a small tax rate on only part of their earnings. They may owe some tax overall throughout the year, but they generally have that amount and a bit more withheld from their paychecks as they go along. So, they generally see a tax refund every year. People in the upper-middle class pay federal income taxes on most of their earnings. The first few thousand of earnings are tax-free for them. The next level of income is at the lowest tax rate. Then, part of their income is in the next highest tax rate, but overall, their average federal income tax burden is generally not much higher than their posted state sales tax rate. If they participate in tax-deferred pensions, like 401(k)s, that money is not taxed when it is earned; the income taxation on that money is deferred until it is withdrawn. They do pay Social Security and Medicare taxes on their wages, bonuses, and self-employment income. In 2016 with four people in a household earning $60,000, about $22,000 would escape income tax, and the remaining $38,000 would be taxed partly at 10% and partly at 15%, for a total tax bill of about $4,772.50, which is an average overall tax rate of almost 8%. This amount plus a bit more is likely withheld from their paychecks throughout the year, providing a modest tax refund yearly. They are subject to Social Security and Medicare taxes on their earnings as well, which is roughly the amount of federal income tax of $4,590.

For people who are in the top 10% of income earners however, the tax rate accelerates, especially on "earned income," which includes wages, bonuses, and self-employment income. Dividends and capital gains from the sale of stock are taxed at a much favored, lower federal income tax rate and are not subject to Social Security. In 2013, the top 1% of earners had about $428,713 in income, per the Statistics of Income provided by the IRS. They had an average federal income tax rate of just over 27%, or about $116,100. So, tax planning becomes a priority. Their tax structure is more complex than those of lower earning people. They are more likely to be using tax deferred pensions. They are more likely to own houses large enough to make it worthwhile to item-ize their deductions. They are more likely to invest in stocks which provide dividends and capital gains at a tax rate of 15–20%, rather than the 33% ordi-nary income rate posted in the tax tables. They only pay Social Security and

Medicare of 7.65% on about the first $118,500 for 2016. After that, their tax rate falls to 1.45%, which represents the Medicare portion of the tax only.

It is at this level of income that average federal income tax rates statistically level off. Those in the top 0.1% make about $1,860,848 and pay almost 1% more in average tax rates (almost 28%), but those in the top 0.01% make about $9,460,540 and pay a lower average tax rate of just about 26.2%, reflecting the shift from earning income to having one's money earn income for them. The falling of tax rates may also reflect the hiring of effective tax planners. And, the falling tax rates have been noticed by the IRS. Millionaires get the most IRS scrutiny, with 9.55% of tax returns audited in 2015. The audit rate jumps to 34.69% of those with incomes of $10 million or more.[219] We need income tax planning, but we also begin to think about estate tax planning and asset protection from greedy people who may try to sue us.

We also understand returns on investment and the time value of money. While the time value of money is used often to calculate the earnings on investments over time, it does help those of us who were fortunate enough to win the lottery decide whether to accept a lump sum or a series of payments.[220]

We still look for deals. However, we're a lot less likely to clip $0.25 coupons on box cake mixes and might get $1 million off of a good investment.

Assets and Liabilities

There is a sustained glut of worldwide cash available for investing, though much of this is coming from abroad because Americans aren't saving much comparatively speaking. Even some of us who are wealthy are frozen out of some hedge funds and private equity firms. Our strategy on assets is to:

1. Protect what we have

2. Grow what we have

3. Pass down what we have

Asset protection is a process of using existing laws to insulate our wealth from risk. Properly done, it is not hiding assets or evading taxes or dodging creditors. We might, for example, insulate our children from having *more* responsibility for an auto accident than poorer would by limiting their access to inherited wealth by placing the wealth in a trust rather than distributing it to them outright. In a traditional trust, a Grantor conveys assets to a Trustee for the benefit of someone else. The trustee manages the assets in accordance with a written trust agreement for the benefit of one or more Beneficiaries, who cannot control those assets. A common trust provision is a "spendthrift" provision, which restricts a Beneficiary from assigning future income or trust assets to creditors. Once the assets are in trust, they are generally protected from future creditors of the Grantor, Trustee and Beneficiaries.

So, placing assets in a trust is beneficial for many of us, but it does not grant us anonymity. Assets are discoverable by capable investigators, and by lawyers through the discovery process when a lawsuit exists. Additionally, trusts may be revocable or irrevocable. Revocable trusts, or "living trusts" can be amended or revoked by the Grantor as long as the Grantor is not incapacitated. However, little asset protection is gained by these trusts, they generally serve solely to keep assets out of probate court once the Grantor dies. Irrevocable trusts may not be amended and properly done, can provide immediate asset protection for the Beneficiaries.

Some states do allow Domestic Asset Protection Trusts which differ from traditional trusts because the Grantor retains the benefit of the trust assets. These trusts are sometimes called "self-settled trusts," and are relatively new in asset protection planning. In part because they are new and not available in all states, there is still some uncertainty that they will be honored in judicial proceedings. These trusts may be particularly vulnerable if the Grantor enters bankruptcy because such proceedings can extend the statute of limitations on the protection of the assets.

A few international jurisdictions like Nevis, the Cook Islands, and Belize offer Offshore Self-Settled Asset Protection Trusts, that when properly established, generally offer more assured protection than domestic trusts, but are still vulnerable, particularly in U.S. jurisdictions that do not recognize self-settled trusts.[221] Where trusts hold assets that are not on U.S. soil, those assets are often outside the reach of U.S. creditors; however, in some cases, a U.S. court may choose to apply its own jurisdiction's laws, including contempt charges, to facilitate access to those assets.

For example, if we hold shares in a corporation within the United States, they may be attached to satisfy a court judgment, whereas shares held overseas are far more difficult to attach. Having our corporate shares attached is especially problematic in closely held companies because the judgment creditor can now vote and may exert significant (and in some cases absolute) influence over the company. This behavior is known as "reverse veil piercing." To prevent such share transfers to outside creditors, we might contract among ourselves to a cross-purchase agreement so that we have the right to purchase shares exposed to a creditor. As shareholders, we might have other shareholder agreements in place to purchase shares from deceased or profoundly disabled shareholders.

To the extent that assets are in the form of real estate, local law may apply, making international trusts of little use. Similarly, if we execute reciprocal trusts, where two people execute trusts making one person the beneficiary of their assets, and the other person makes the first person the beneficiary of their assets, those "reciprocal trusts" may be ignored using substance over form analysis where the settlors are in about the same economic position as they were before the trusts.

We also consider protecting our family assets from people marrying into the family, especially with the fragility of marriage in current times. Prenuptial ("prenup") and in some cases postnuptial ("postnup") agreements are considered because our families want to protect their assets. A prenup is a written contract entered into by two people prior to getting married. This contract generally lists the property and debts owned by each prospective spouse and specifies the property rights of each prospective spouse will be if the marriage fails. These agreements clarify financial responsibilities during and shortly after a marriage ends. A postnup agreement is similar, but it is signed by both spouses after marriage or civil union. While we are not yet extremely wealthy, we might want a prenup to pass separate property to our individual children from prior marriages when we die. Without a prenup, our spouse might inherit a large portion of what was our separate property even if they don't need it, and ultimately then pass that property plus their own separate property to their children from a prior marriage, leaving our children with little or nothing. Alimony may be specified in a prenup, as well as how property will be divided in the event of a divorce. And, where one spouse has unfortunate debts, the prenup can be used to protect the assets of the non-debtor spouse.

Where no prenup is inexistence, state laws determine who owns the property acquired during marriage and what happens to that property at divorce, or where there is no will, at death. Normally, under state law, spouses have the right to share ownership of property acquired during marriage.[222] We also have the responsibility to pay our spouse's debts incurred during the marriage. Even so, discussions about prenuptial agreements can be awkward.

Discussing postnuptial agreements can be even more awkward because we are already bound in marriage. We might enter a postnup to divide assets and provide for spousal support in the event of a divorce. Assets that one party brought into the marriage or were subsequently inherited may be especially sensitive, and we might also be sensitive where one spouse has been financially irresponsible, or the target of legal trouble. When a spouse makes substantial career sacrifices to stay at home to care for family members, a postnuptial agreement could provide them with the promise of financial resources should the marriage end. Another reason we might enter in to a postnup is to waive our spousal rights when one of us dies, superseding a will or state laws, especially where there are children from previous relationships that we want taken care of. Postnups can be a template for a separation agreement, including provisions for child custody and child support.

To be enforceable, postnuptial agreements must generally be written and voluntary rather than coerced. Unfair or unconscionable agreements are generally not enforceable. In particular, postnups that restrict, or limit child support or child custody are suspect. Each spouse must make a full and fair disclosure of their assets, liabilities, and income. To be enforceable, postnups must follow the laws of the state where the couple resides. Usually, this means in part that both spouses' signatures must be notarized.

In addition to protecting assets, we want our assets to earn money for us, like little round-the-clock, unpaid workers would do. We grow what we have through prudent investing. Where feasible, we borrow money at less than we receive in return on investment, thus also making money on other people's money. Low interest loans are our friend, especially when we're purchasing assets, and it's hard for us to pay for assets when we can finance them at deep discount rates.

However, we choose our loans carefully to ensure they're true friends that don't hurt us. For example, we research our credit card rates and fees, but also the benefits. We compare them to our lifestyle to make sure that we choose appropriately.

Loans can actually help us protect some of our assets by making them less attractive to potential creditors and predators. For example, where we take out a legitimate mortgage on real property rather than paying cash for that property, there is not much equity in that property, and creditors (other than the lienholder) generally will not foreclose on an asset from which they cannot bleed off cash. When we take out a mortgage on property in which we already own and have a substantial equity interest, this technique is known as "equity stripping." The proceeds are then invested in other protected assets such as an annuity, retirement fund, or personal homestead. We might also want to equity strip an asset that is not earning much money to finance more productive investments.

We commonly have access to lines of credit. All of this credit is risky though. While we have more income, we're spending more personally, and often much of that is on credit. Add that to the business risks we're taking, and we are often just as "on the financial edge" as many of our lower-income friends. Some of us seem to get hooked on the adrenalin of that risky life style, and sometimes when we take unprotected risks, we lose. But, when we do accumulate wealth, we can't take it with us.

Once we have grown and protected our assets, we begin to think about transferring them when we die, and maybe even to some extent before we die. We consult with attorneys to develop wealth transfer plans. These plans may include some combination of gifting before death, as well as the structure of wills for distribution of our assets upon our passing. The U.S. tax code does not tax small gifts, which is $15,000 per recipient per year, as of 2018. If we are married, we can use a gift-splitting technique that allows both ourselves and our spouses to gift $15,000 per recipient per year, for a total of $30,000 per year per recipient. The $30,000 per year can come from one spouse's funds, provided that the other spouse consents to the gift. If we are married and have three children, we can effectively shelter $90,000 per year; and if each of those children are married, we can shelter up to $180,000 per year by gifting to our children's spouses as well.

We investigate establishing charitable foundations, which are nonprofit entities formed to make grants to unrelated organizations, institutions, or individuals for scientific, educational, cultural, religious, or other charitable purposes.[223] We may form a family foundation in which our family members endow the foundation and participate in its management.

Where we own a business, we may choose to gift company merchandise or services, sometimes contributing employee paid time to volunteer for causes. When planning to pass our wealth to family members, we may give ownership shares rather than the money itself. We hire lawyers to help us pass down nonvoting, appreciating ownership shares to our grown children or our minor children in trust. We want nonvoting shares because, while we want to limit the size of our estate subject to tax, we may not yet be willing to give up control of our companies. We want to gift appreciating ownership shares because the value of these shares will grow tax-free until sold. By keeping the depreciating assets in our estate and gifting the assets that are going up in value, we keep our estate smaller over time than it would have been had we given depreciating assets. When the ownership shares are sold, they will likely be taxed at a lower, long-term capital gains tax rate.

Business Interests

We understand that we must take risks, but also understand that we've got to mitigate those risks. We are increasingly less averse to failure. When we buy businesses, we include non-compete agreements and other employment agreements. We are entrepreneurs on an international scale, planning around suppliers and customers on a global level. Accordingly, our tax planning considers global implications. We may consider forming a foreign corporation, but these rules can be complex, adding unnecessary costs to running a business. Foreign corporations may provide some protection against U.S. judgements.

We also routinely use multiple entities to protect business assets. If we own multiple business properties, they may well be in multiple LLCs so that an incident at one property does not expose the other properties to loss. Where a business is especially susceptible to legal claims, the associated assets are often held in a separate company. For example, restaurants could serve food bought in good faith that contains E. coli, leading the company to be sued. If we own that restaurant along with the building and land used for the restaurant, it makes sense for the building and land to be in one company, which then leases the premises to the restaurant business which we hold as a separate company. If E. coli comes, we may lose our restaurant business, but we don't lose our building and land in which we may have tied up quite a bit of wealth.

Where we (and our spouse, if applicable) are the sole owner(s) of each LLC, the LLC is a "disregarded entity" for tax purposes, meaning that we can file them with our 1040, rather than filing a separate tax return for each property. If we have enough properties to warrant a consolidated management company, that company will be set up as an LLC as well, so that any liability incurred by the management company does not expose all the individual properties that are being managed.

We may have even compared the different state rules for forming an LLC to find the most protective LLC for our business. For example, in some states like Florida, if a creditor were to attach our distributions from an LLC, they would have to pay the taxes on the share of taxable profits and losses on that ownership interest.[224] Similarly, some states offer a "series LLC" to attempt to help us efficiently run multiple LLCs. The state allows the owners of a series LLC to own only one LLC, while at the same time statutorily segregating assets and their related liabilities into different groups.[225] The debts associated with one series are collectable only against the assets held by that series. New series units may be added efficiently to that one LLC. Because the legal and tax complexity of a series LLC is formidable (but generally not as complex as individual LLCs), we consult with our team of lawyers, accountants, perhaps bankers, and insurance agents to set this up.

Sometimes, the advice from our professionals is to form a foreign LLC, often in the Caribbean. The advantage to such capital formation is that if the foreign LLC becomes subject to a U.S. judgment, the creditor must often use the foreign law to reach the LLC assets. Some jurisdictions have the strong reputation of being pro-debtor, discouraging such foreign suits by creditors. Protection is enhanced when the LLC is managed by a non-U.S. resident, individual, or company with no ties to the U.S. and funded with foreign assets.[226] However, where a U.S. debtor refuses to return foreign LLC assets to the U.S. for collection, the debt may be enforced by incarcerating the debtor.

Getting from Here to Uber-Rich

We need to avoid key financial mistakes, which are sometimes based on emotions rather than objectivity. For example, when people inherit wealth, they sometimes act too quickly, while they are still grief-stricken. One author gave an example of an heir abruptly quitting a job before figuring out if the inheritance would last for their lifetime.[227] Another example is where heirs fail to seek professional help and buy the wrong products, or cash out annuities without understanding the tax consequences.[228]

We have succeeded, but we may want to financially succeed even more. We may be driven by the challenge of making money, or by greed itself. We may also be driven by the fear of failing, as in the saying, "easy come, easy go." Hence, there may never be enough.

For those of us who are not driven by greed or fear, we probably just think about money differently. According to self-made millionaire Steve Siebold, wealthy people often use the following mental tricks:[229]

1. We believe in financial abundance, in freedom, and in unlimited opportunity. We believe that there's always more money out there, even though we might not have it right now.

2. We set "unrealistically high" expectations. We often don't realize these expectations, but we come a lot closer to achieving them than if we hadn't set these expectations.

3. We are proactive. We live by mottos like "champions don't wait for things to happen, they make things happen."

4. We think of making money as a game. The more money we make, the more we "win" the game.

5. We think of money as a friend or ally. It helps our family. It works for us while we sleep. It helps us achieve our non-financial goals. It buys us a certain amount of freedom.

6. More than most, we block out fear and are willing to leave our comfort zone. We take measured risks. We are aware of the risks we are taking, and work to mitigate the downside exposure to those risks, but we take the risks anyway.

7. We learn to perform in an environment of ongoing uncertainty.

That is, we have a different mindset than we had when we were poorer.

Is This Good Enough?

America is minting more millionaire retirees than ever, if we include the value of our homes.[230] The share of people who are millionaires has doubled since 1989.[231] However, many of us millionaires are retirees. Content with our financial condition, we opt not to work for more money, and additionally continue to spend at or below our standard of living we had when we were working. We recognize that being high-profile, yet alone famous, brings with it certain risks to our safety and wealth. We have dropped out of climbing the socioeconomic ladder in favor of boat drinks and bingo.

This *is* enough money for some of us. We have no need to show off or be perceived as especially wealthy. For example, Brian Portnoy, a behavioral finance expert, asserts that the idea of wealth, truly defined, is funded contentment.[232] Wealth and the financial decisions that build wealth are interwoven with a joyful, meaningful life. Wealth is hollow without self-awareness.

With sufficient self-awareness though, we recognize that there's nothing wrong with wanting more money still, and some of us do. Those of us who aspire to more may still try to avoid notice. We have begun paying for privacy.

We vacation at quiet resorts with strong security. We join private clubs that limit photography. We are cautious of those we don't know because we know we have it well and that others would pretend to have money to have access to our wealth and connections.

In some cases, however, pursuing more money at this level and the next can be dysfunctional or even a "behavioral addiction."[233] More commonly known behavioral addictions are shopaholism, gambling, sex, and extreme overeating; these can change the brain chemistry similar to the mood changing effects of alcohol or drugs. These compulsive behaviors can lead to negative consequences, including shattered relationships.

How Much, If at All, Should We Change Those Assumptions?

At this level, self-awareness is critical to our evolving. With that self-awareness, we may be simultaneously pleased with what we have, and enjoying the challenge of making money, much like it is a game. But, it is important to have clear goals for a balanced life at this stage, otherwise our problems might only be exasperated with more money.

How Might We Best Help Those in Need?

We have resources that can make a life better for the people of our choice. We can afford to "vacation for a cause."[234] We can help organize and support galas and parties for hospitals, homeless shelters, schools, and to fight diseases. We must develop the skills to make sure that the money raised is used properly, but we have the skills and education to do so. We are in a good place.

CHAPTER 9

When Millionaire Just Isn't Enough—
Middle-Upper to Upper-Upper Class

"A million dollars isn't cool. You know what's cool? A billion dollars."[235]

———

Much less is published about the people in this group, and that is by our own design. We pay for privacy, and many of our transactions, including large real estate transactions, are made in cash. Traditionally, we went to many of the same schools and clubs and married within that social structure. Family lineage ("breeding") and pedigree mattered. However, wealth has shifted over the last half century making these rules less applicable.

Many of us actually see ourselves as "simple, middle-class people who just got lucky after a lot of hard work."[236] But, with respect to our work, we identify with an international, cosmopolitan, economic elite that often serve on boards of foreign and multinational companies and have global social networks.[237]

Life at this Level: The Rules Are Different for Us

We operate largely in our own parallel world. Robert Frank estimated that even back in 2004, the richest 1% of Americans were earning more than the total national incomes of France, Italy, or Canada.[238] We are flexible with what country's currency we use to pay. Travel is an ordinary activity, and it's common that our favorite restaurant is in a foreign country. A concierge or personal assistant from our team books most of the travel arrangements using services such as Net Jets, taking us to destination clubs, where there are no lines for a ski lift and no tee times on the golf course. We have a household manager. We also have standing relationships with a florist, caterers, a domestic employment service, hairdresser, tailor, personal physicians, personal shoppers, in-house chef, childcare services, and a personal trainer. Many or all of these helpers come to our home or office instead of the other way around. Similarly, we hire holiday house decorations and event staff for all parties and holidays. We have multiple houses, perhaps in multiple countries, and they are staffed. We have more cars than drivers, and often travel either on a private plane or first class. We have spent time on a yacht. We often travel internationally and may have reserved travel to space.

We have servants everywhere, so there's less personal space, and we realize that we are a high value target for people who want our time, money, and talents. This had led even politicians like President Obama to declare "no new friends" upon entering the White House. Social activity often takes place in private clubs and associations, many of which may ban cameras formally (but often have a photo booth for fun); all of which discourage them because privacy is paramount. We seek out private, members only clubs where we can both socialize with others who have similar problems and avoid those who may be seeking to socialize strictly for their own gain. We understand when our friends at this level complain about friends and family from other socioeconomic levels asking for a business or personal loan. Those changes in our relationship dynamics can make us lonely.

Being super rich can be lonely, because as a character in Jonathan Franzen's latest novel _Purity_ says, "people around you constantly project themselves onto you....t's as if you're not even there as a person. You're merely an object that people project their idealism onto, or their anger, or what have you. [And] if you try to talk about [the perils of being rich and famous], some young woman in Oakland, California will accuse you of self-pity." [239]

To some extent, we believe that economic inequality represents just desserts. [240] And, the more economic inequality that we see in our own country, the more we believe that meritocracy is working properly. [241] We are more likely to see class as inherent and fixed, and more likely to see the world as a just, fair place. [242]

We do fly our jets to attend public events like the Superbowl and complain about the crowded parking for those jets. When traveling, we use the private airport security and ultra-private lounges, not the TSA lines and airport lounges. For some entertainment, like theme parks, we can reserve the entire park after-hours for our entourage.

We can meet nearly anyone in the world. [243] However, we have maintained many "friendships" with people we do not like, but who are in our same social class and have suitable connections. We are more likely to view relationships in terms of strategic exchanges. For example, when explaining our reasons for divorce, we are more likely to report differences in value systems, partners' excessive demands, our own self-interest, and general incompatibility than are reported by poorer friends. [244]

Our social invitations still arrive in paper form. We require prenuptial agreements. We hire domestic staff that are loyal and maintain confidentiality. We do not use our real names when we check into public hotels and have "screens" that keep unwanted people at a distance. Our children are in the preferred private schools and sometimes boarding schools as early as age six. [245] We have personal family physicians that also make house calls, and in situations where there are chronic health problems, they may live on-site. Health is important, but we have the best health care possible, so we tend to take health for granted. We do tend to be germaphobes. Life is good, and we want to live forever. Germs threaten that. We have attorneys and accountants on retainer, if not on staff.

We share our houses with this group and may build something of a compound to keep our friends and family close. However, in designing that compound, a private location is key. Our wealth may be published in magazines, but it should not be seen from the street.

Not only do we share our houses and jets, there's rarely an argument in our group about who picks up a tab. Any of us can, and most of us do. Freebies and other incentives to win our business are the norm. That is, while we monitor the big picture money closely, the day-to-day money tends to be immaterial to us and does not factor into our daily decisions. However, we do expect those who work for us to be mindful of the smaller, regularly occurring costs of running a business, or our household.

We contribute to several political campaigns from local to national and international levels in part to protect our wealth interests. These interests are different than those of middle America, though.

For example, while most of middle America solidly agrees with the statement, "[m]inimum wage should be high enough so that no family with a full-time worker falls below the official poverty line," less than half of the elite agree with this statement. And, unlike the majority of middle Americans, the majority of us also favor cuts to domestic programs like Medicare, education, and highways in order to reduce the federal deficit. We are also more tolerant of U.S. companies setting up overseas than middle America.[246] Because we can fund elections, our voices are heard and are perhaps disproportionately influential through the candidates that we endorse. We want access to political players on demand as needed and will ask for political favors as we think are prudent. As a heavy contributor, it's common that we are awarded with an ambassadorship or honorary political position that converges with our interest, like chancellor of a public university system.

We serve on the boards of charities. Charitable activities, often paired with an attitude of noblesse oblige, which as defined by Merriam-Webster's Dictionary as, "the obligation of honorable, generous, and responsible behavior associated with high rank or birth,"[247] take on a larger role. We frequently merge charitable and business events through corporate sponsorship and attendance. Similarly, media management and political activities are often merged with business. We have boxes for sporting events and artistic events. We buy original art from specific artists, often paying a million dollars or more. We look critically for items with artistic merit with which to surround ourselves.

We have a reputation supported by academic research that shows that we are more likely to exhibit unethical or self-serving behaviors, including cheating, lying, taking valuable goods from children, and driving in violation of the law.[248] For example, in one academic study, about half of drivers in the highest status vehicles drove illegally through a crosswalk as a pedestrian was waiting to cross versus none in the lowest status vehicles.[249] Another researcher asserted that those successfully working on Wall Street have a much higher percentage rate of sociopaths than that of the general population.[250] We are less likely to be sensitive to the needs of others, and less able to read others' facial expressions, but that may be because we are less likely to be threatened by other, violent people, so this skill is not as important to us.[251] Then again, less sensitivity is true of people who have *fake* money. University of Berkeley research found that when two students played Monopoly with one having been given much more money than the other, the richer player acted more aggressively after an initial discomfort period.[252] However, like the students in the study, we relearn connection and compassion easily when that is the focus of our attention.[253]

Wealth has even been linked to addiction. Academic studies have found that our children are more vulnerable to substance abuse, and attribute that tendency to the high pressure to achieve and the isolation from our parents.[254] Wealth may shield us from worrying about whether our electricity will be turned off or whether we can afford enough groceries for the week, but it does not exempt our children from adjustment problems. Because the world accommodates us on many occasions, we might even find it harder to adjust than if we were poor.

All of this tends to paint an unlikeable picture of us, and indeed, some of those with much less money find our wealth to be morally offensive. In truth, we are no better or worse than others would be in our situation, and perhaps than others are generally. As one author wrote, "[m]oney is like a truth serum. It brings out people's true nature. So, if someone's already a jerk, they become more of a jerk after they're rich."[255]

And, we are among the most effectively charitable people, in part because we have the wherewithal to be charitable, and in part because we have a keen grasp of organizational effectiveness, and having given money to a cause, we follow up to make sure that those contributions are effective in achieving results. Many of us believe that "with great wealth comes great responsibility." If a cause touches our heart, we make epic changes to the community and the world. Both John D. Rockefeller and Andrew Carnegie gave away millions in the last decades of their lives.[256] For example, Andrew Carnegie funded over 2,800 libraries, as well as a museum and university in Pittsburgh, Pennsylvania. At the time of his death, he had given away 90% of his fortune.[257] He has written, "He who dies rich, dies disgraced."[258] Rockefeller built the University of Chicago and Rockefeller University in New York. However, Rockefeller's motives are sometimes attributed to fending off attacks on his monopoly, Standard Oil.[259]

While we are charitable, we exercise our compassion differently from our ancestors. We are more likely to give away money while we are alive so that we can watch it do good. We demand accountability, and we can often do that with our own foundations or smaller funds than with larger, more established charities that we sometimes perceive have too much overhead, and are more concerned with self-perpetuation than actual charitable results.

Any problem that money can solve, is solved for us. We are free to be ourselves without having to conform to the expectations of others; we generally have a coherent self-view.[260] Some would say that we tend to be entitled and narcissistic.[261]

That does provide some of us with a false sense of security that in turn leads some of us to disregard common ethics and laws. For example, in 2015, a 16-year-old boy claimed in his manslaughter trial that his family's wealth should exempt him from responsibility for a drunk driving accident which resulted in the deaths of four people. This was dubbed the "affluenza defense," where affluenza, as defined by the Merriam-Webster Dictionary, is:

> the unhealthy and unwelcome psychological and social effects of <u>affluence</u> regarded especially as a widespread societal problem, such as:

> a. feelings of guilt, lack of motivation, and social isolation experienced by wealthy people

> b. extreme materialism and consumerism associated with the pursuit of wealth and success and resulting in a life of chronic dissatisfaction, debt, overwork, stress, and impaired relationships[262]

In this defense, Psychologist G. Dick Miller argued that because the boy suffered from affluenza, he may not have fully comprehended the consequences of his actions.[263] Wealth has been linked to other psychological and sociological problems as well. Extremely affluent people have been shown to experience higher rates of depression.[264] Striving for materialism has been linked with lower relationship satisfaction.[265] We are very used to the material comforts that we have, and compare them to other comforts that we have experienced as well as the possessions of others in what psychologists call a "hedonic treadmill," and others call "taking it all for granted." Yet, we are extremely good at building wealth, even when compared to other, poorer millionaires.[266]

Earning the appreciation and respect of others, and of course love, are what makes us happy. We also want to realize our personal potential.[267] Having our material needs met means that we are free to pursue deeper meaning. We find meaning in providing employment to thousands. We find meaning in making products that make others' lives better. We can find meaning in the charities we have supported.

In the words of entrepreneur and billionaire Marc Benioff, "Nothing is going to make you feel better. Philanthropy is *absolutely* the best drug I've ever taken."[268]

Income and Expenses

We are adept at reading financial statements and actually run something of a profit and loss statement and balance sheet for our household but have other people that prepare them for us. Our family's college funds are funded, if they need to be funded at all, and it is assumed we will pursue an Ivy League education. Managing money is done by professional lawyers, accountants, and international advisers. We review this information on at least a monthly basis but have the electronic tools to monitor tenuous situations more closely. Many of our advisers are on retainer. Overseeing corporate property and membership on boards of directors are common items on our to do list. We hold stock certificates, property deeds, trust documents, and our pricey artwork has provenance.[269]

Our revenue sources increasingly include more investments, which are taxed at a lower rate than other ordinary income and escape most Social Security and Medicare taxes altogether, although we are often paid for our services, especially as consultants. Our investments might be from our savings, but likely we have a trust fund managed by dedicated financial advisers. When we do own businesses in which we are actively involved, we do not take on the role of traditional entrepreneur, who would wake up early every morning and be involved in each critical detail of managing the business throughout the day. Instead, we choose from several investment offers (and we counter-offer), and check in on the broader, big picture strategies from time to time. Having several of these and always seeking more keeps us very busy. If we are famous, we may lend our name to products and services that others produce in return for periodic payments and an equity stake. People pay us for access to our connections when we let them. So, we are more interdependent than independent, which is difficult for us if we have moved up through the economic ladder rather than having been born into it. We frequently are paid to serve on boards of directors for our own companies and those of our associates, and we invite them to sit on our boards as well. We vote ourselves raises frequently.[270] Since our revenue sources are intertwined with that of our family and friends, who we can trust becomes paramount. And, we actively seek to keep a comfortable fortune within the family and a set of close friends that we rely upon most.

Of our expenses, we spend much more on security, convenience, and privacy than most. We fly in private jets which typically cost $3,500 per hour, so we can come and go largely on our schedule, passing through private security lines and waiting in private security lounges for our party. We generally fly nonstop. We can use smaller, private airports that often get us physically closer to our desired destination. The food and other services and perhaps the plane itself are catered to our tastes. Compared to first class fares, flying this way costs more, but not necessarily that much more, especially considering the value, or what we earn, for our time.

We view tax planning as an international challenge, and we hire a team of professionals to organize our business interests to take full advantage of the tax laws across nations and local jurisdictions. We incorporate our charitable giving into our tax planning. While the spirit of philanthropy itself drives the charitable contribution, how we give and what else we hope to achieve becomes important.[271] We may give as part of our family identity and as an expression of our family values. We may give to create a legacy. We may give to create political capital in the community. We may give in a way that closely dovetails with wealth management because we often give in conjunction with a company that we control and because corporate giving can demonstrate a commitment to long-term goals[272] and enhance our corporate reputation.[273] We may give because we are socially responsible and expect that we can make a change in society. Although, we give carefully and with much consideration to avoid bogus requests for money.

Where we own businesses, we may engage in "enterprise philanthropy,"[274] a way of funding charities through an intersection of family, business, and society. We may form a corporate foundation that is a separate legal entity from the corporation and independently governed, but which maintains close ties with the corporation.[275]

We may have our own family foundation, and participate in its management, or have donor advised funds, where we fund money into a public foundation, but consult on how those funds are spent. We may make a sizeable endowment to a nonprofit organization for its ongoing support. We may have one or more charitable trusts that dovetail with our tax planning.

Two such trusts are a charitable remainder trust and a charitable lead trust. In a charitable remainder trust, we normally make a gift of investments to a charity, immediately triggering a potential tax deduction, but we reserve the income from the contribution for life. The income may come in the form of a fixed dollar amount each year, called a "charitable remainder annuity trust," or a percentage of the value of the assets, called a "charitable remainder unitrust." If the trust sells part of the investments, the gains are not taxable. When we die, the investments pass outright to the charity, bypassing our estate, and thus estate taxes. A charitable lead trust is a gift for a fixed period of years, with the income from the trust after assets are sold going to the charity. Once the term expires, for example, once our grandchildren reach the age of majority, whatever is left in the trust is passed directly to our grandchildren or other family members. In this trust as well, the investments are also excluded from our estate.

Assets and Liabilities

Our wealth may have been made by us or the person possessing it or passed down through the family. An estimated 80% of assets come from transfers from prior generations, not from current income. We have established trust funds for our children at birth. Those who receive their wealth this way are sometimes referred to as "old money." People with old money sometimes act differently than those with "new money," which is wealth earned by the person possessing it. While we tend to believe that there's no specific amount of money will make us happy, rather, "the more, the better."[276] And, most of us believe we'd need at least 500% more money than we currently have, in order to be perfectly happy.[277] Less than 13% believe we could achieve perfect happiness with the extensive wealth that we already have.[278] It takes at least $8 million before we are happier than a somewhat poorer brethren, and even then, we're only slightly happier.[279] Our attitude toward money does depend in part on how we got our money. Millionaires who made their wealth rather than inheriting it *were* happier than those who didn't.[280]

Taking on debt is just another part of business. We may choose to fund projects ourselves or with those partners we like. We have enough family funds to fund an ad hoc family bank for loaning to friends and relatives, which cuts the larger banks out of the interest profits. We might even own some smaller banks themselves.

When we have so much, we have so much to lose. To protect ourselves, our business interests become much more complex. We place our equity interests in a protective partnership or LLC so that outside creditors cannot acquire voting interests in our assets. Creditors can place a "charging order" on debt-or-partners, however.[281] The charging order is essentially a lien that entitles the creditor to company non-liquidating distributions, if any. However, charging orders generally cannot be used to involuntarily transfer voting rights, and where the LLC is a closely controlled company, the lack of distributions may be sufficient incentive for a settlement of less than the judgment rendered by the courts.

Even if we keep our wealth, we are mortal and can't take it with us. We wrestle with the question of how much we should pass on to our children and grandchildren. While 68% of millennials expect an inheritance, only about 40% will receive one.[282] Some billionaires—especially self-made billionaires—are on record as leaving most of their wealth to charities, not children.[283] Reasons for this decision vary.

Bill Gates explains, "[i]t's not a favor to kids to have them have huge sums of wealth. It distorts anything they might do, creating their own path."[284] Warren Buffett explains that he wants to leave his kids "enough money so that they would feel they could do anything, but not so much that they could do nothing."[285] Michael Bloomberg writes, "[i]f you want to do something for your children and show them how much you love them, the single best thing—by far—is to support organizations that will create a better world for them and their children."[286]

What Now? There's More to Life Than Money

One behavioral finance expert, Brian Portnoy, believes that the true definition of wealth is "funded contentment," and that funded contentment allows us to underwrite a meaningful life. That is, over focusing on becoming extremely financially rich does not lead to a better life than we can have at most lower levels of financial life.[287]

But, what makes a joyful life? The key, Portnoy believes, is self-awareness and striking a balance between pushing for more and being content with enough.[288] He promotes the idea that to have true wealth, we must have a life where purpose and practice are thoughtfully calibrated.

CHAPTER 10

What Happens When Wealth Goes Down, Either by Chance or through Planning?

"I wasn't worth a cent two years ago, and now I owe two million dollars."[289]

It only takes one mistake, or one major life event for fortunes to reverse at least temporarily, and the lower we start on the economic ladder, the smaller the mistake need be. This could be because an individual loses a job or capacity to work, an economic shock to the family (medical, casualty, marital), or due to a broader economic downturn (great recession, great depression).

- Connie's[290] husband provided a life estate when he died in the condo that he owned and furnished for her. With her Social Security check and a paid condo, she should be able to live comfortably for the rest of her days, he reasoned. However, the attorney drew up the paper work for the condo, never specifying that the furnishings and appliances were included. In an alleged attempt to push Connie out of the condo sooner, his children allegedly tried to take all of the furniture and appliances from the condo, leaving Connie financially strapped to replace them.

- Diedre enjoyed every puff of every cigarette she ever smoked. Now she has COPD, and her medical costs combined with her inability to work leave her financially drained.

- Jonah and Kathy had a low six-figure income, easily supporting their three children until one of them got cancer. Between the costs of travel for specialists, the time missed from work, the extra childcare costs, and the medical bills, they are in danger of losing their house and their jobs.

- Frank worked for the same company for 32 years, when it was closed suddenly.

- Mara retired and received a pension to supplement her Social Security, easily affording retirement—until the pension plan went bankrupt and just stopped paying out.

- Jenna invested with an advertised financial professional—who was later investigated by the state for financial improprieties. Her hard-earned nest egg was depleted by what appeared to be a financial professional.

- Justin did not believe that he could successfully complete four-year college degree, but the job market for those without a degree had weakened. Like about 12% of prime-age men, he had trouble finding a full-time job with a salary and benefits above the poverty line.[291]

- Even simple retirement from work, a reasoned life choice, could cause our income to go down.

Financial reversals have been happening more frequently than in previous generations. Wealth is more easily earned, but it is also more easily lost, as illustrated by the Dot.com bust, the real estate bust, and financial recession. In one study of Americans between 1969-2011, a full 70% earned enough to be in the top 20% of earners, and nearly 80% dropped at least temporarily near or below the poverty line or they were compelled to access social safety net programs like food stamps or unemployment benefits.[292] It is predicted that more than half of working age Americans will experience at least one year near the poverty line.[293] Many people have experienced life at up and down nearly the whole range of the socioeconomic ladder.[294] Hopefully, when we fall, we stop the slide and also reinforce our strength at the level we are at, beginning the climb again with new transcending behaviors.

Life at a Lower Level Than Before—"I Used to Have Money One Time."[295]

When our fortunes reverse, we know we should adjust, beginning with discretionary expenses and working into a long-term change plan that considers both raising revenue and cutting long-term expenses. We scale back on vacations or cut vacations. We may move to a smaller house with a lower mortgage or move in with family or friends for short time periods. We reconfigure our eating patterns, eating out less often and choosing more modest meals when we prepare them ourselves. We suspend unnecessary purchases, including clothing. We make these changes during the interim as most of us also plan to rise back up again.

None of this is easy. Some say it can't be done. One expert put it this way, "(people) will maintain (their quality of life) at any cost until they can't."[296] Yet, people rise every day.

Stopping the fall takes willpower, which is a skill set that works like a muscle in that the harder it works, the more tired it gets, leaving less willpower for other things.[297] And, willpower is not the only problem to overcoming financial obstacles. The societal effect of being poorer is that the quality of our decisions goes down. This happens to each of us. Under the stress of scarcity, our IQ actually falls, and our decisions get worse until our situation gets turned around., Unintentionally, we are in our own way in the fight to rise.[298] Our pride is also wounded. While people in generational poverty may feel that the world owes us a living, those of us in situational poverty may be too proud to seek or accept charity.[299] We may go through Elisabeth Kubler-Ross' five stages of grief: denial, anger, bargaining, depression, and acceptance.[300]

When this happens to us when we were in the middle class, hope and choice are replaced with fear and scarcity, and our ability to reason and see options suffers. It is worse for us who see ourselves as the main provider for our household. We may see the setbacks as a personal failing, so we often hide the problem. Middle class people tend not to talk about money or money problems.

There are unwritten middle-class rules of money: "I don't ask you for money, and you don't ask me," and "if you borrow money, you have to pay it back."[301] There's also a social cost regardless of where we fell from: we lose friends. We are embarrassed when we can't afford to socialize like we used to, and friends are afraid that inviting us to something costly may make us feel embarrassed. And, society has little pity. This is especially true if we were wealthy, when others may actually relish in our struggles because many in society perceive us as "evil."[302]

When assessing what to do when fortunes reverse, we must identify if the reverse in fortunes is deliberate and predictable, as when we retire or drop out of the rat race, or whether the reversal was unpredictable.

Retirement and Predictable Reverses—"You Can Take This Job and Shove It"[303]

In planning for a reversal, we have some choice in how we distribute our current income between spending and savings. We can scale back now, so that we are not scaling back as much in retirement.[304] Scaling back early is important to an easier retirement because we can live not only on what we saved, but on what those savings earned. Still, many of us have nest eggs that are inadequate for our desired retirement. According to one poll, 27% of those surveyed had no retirement savings, and another 22% have less than $100,000—that's nearly half of us.[305] Similarly, an AICPA poll found that nearly half of us fear that we will never be able to retire.[306] And, because we've lived through the Great Recession, our ability to save was impaired as we waited for our pre-recession earning power to recover.

Budgeting for our retirement is often difficult, because our spending throughout retirement is likely not constant. We may want to catch up on travel and social activities initially, but as that slows, health care expenses may increase. With uncertainty comes fear.[307] Assuming that we do have retirement savings, we can consult with reputable investment firms that can give us a fresh, objective plan for making our savings last. For example, investment advisers may tell us to sell down the shares of stock in our portfolio in favor of more cash, bonds, or a bond ladder, which is a series of bonds that mature predictably to provide steady income. While following this advice means that our portfolio earnings may drop, we are protected from market swings which could brutalize our retirement budget. We may also be advised to convert some of our investments into annuities that provide a guaranteed income to reduce the risk of market swings that we would have to cover if we remained invested there. Investment advisers are also trained to account for economic factors and health care and Social Security cost uncertainty. We might consider a reverse mortgage.

A reverse mortgage is a loan against the home equity that we've built up over time. We borrow against the value of our home and can receive money as a lump sum, fixed monthly payment, or line of credit. The loan is due when we die, move away or sell our home. Because this is a loan, the proceeds are not taxable, and we retain title to the property, although the home is used as collateral for the mortgage. Unlike normal loans, there are generally not required levels of income or minimum credit scores to qualify. We no longer have to make house payments; however, we do have to keep current with property taxes and insurance that are normally included in a house payment's monthly escrow. We also have to pay monthly mortgage insurance. We must maintain the property in good shape. Protections against additional estate debt are in place in case the home drops in value. However, these loans can be costly, and have a history of being fraught with scammers.

Importantly, preparing for retirement requires an entirely different mindset.[308] We do not have the same income flow. We have more time to enjoy sometimes expensive pleasures that eluded us or were scaled back while we were working. We have less time in our future to plan for, or to safety net bad decisions. We are switching from a savings mindset to a spending mindset and no longer seeing our investment balances rise—we are no longer spending less than we earn! We must take only what we have and make it last forever. Some of us have guaranteed pension, but most of us our on our own to ensure our monthly income in retirement. Our parents may be of little help, as they are more likely to have had guaranteed pensions than we are.

Behavioral academics recommend thinking of our expense budget as five buckets of money:

1. Necessities like housing, transportation, personal items, some small entertainment budget just to offset stress and taxes

2. Health care expenses

3. Emergencies

4. Fun money

5. Bequests to our heirs

To fund these buckets, we can use two buckets of income: guaranteed sources of income like Social Security and lifetime annuities, and return on other investments, like IRAs.

If we can meet our necessities budget and health care budget on the guaranteed income amount, we should always be okay, provided we have a reasonable amount of savings for emergencies. Then, we can spend the return on other investments for fun and leave the balance of those accounts to bury us and leave to our heirs.

Preparing for our retirement may also mean minimizing our debt, because we may need the open line of credit for future emergencies if we cannot quickly get additional sources of income. Of course, finance charges on loans and credit cards are also a consideration if we owe significant debt going into retirement.

Unpredictable Reverses—"If It Weren't for Bad Luck, I'd Have No Luck at All"[309]

Sometimes scaling back is not a choice. Sometimes we are forced into retirement.[310] We may have cosigned for student loans, and find that our children or grandchildren have defaulted, resulting in a garnishment to our Social Security payments.[311] Economic recessions hit, and we may find ourselves unemployed or employed at much less income than we previously made. Fallout from economic recessions create psychological losses as well as financial ones.[312] We are in good company. According to one study, 96% of Americans experience at least four income shocks in their working years, and over 60% of workers went at least one year without income by age 70.[313] These losses are scarring. Where there are higher unemployment benefits however, there is a higher national well-being.[314]

Assets and Liabilities

We put aside a little money where we can by using tools like email and text reminders to save as we get paid. In one study, those who set a monthly reminder to save increased their savings by 6%.[315]

Where there is no money to save and we are still short, we begin to draw down any liquid savings that we may have, followed by shorter-term investments like stocks and bonds. One setback alone does not normally hurt our retirement savings much, but repeated or chronic problems do.[316] When there is no more liquid cash, we may charge bills to revolving charge accounts. It is tempting to raid our retirement savings,[317] although this source of cash is generally taxed as income when withdrawn, sometimes with an extra 10% penalty on top of the tax is what is deemed an "early withdrawal," because we are not yet 59½ years old and we are withdrawing the funds without a permissible purpose. The poorer we are, the more we take from retirement savings in a crisis. Wealthy people fund these times from other sources of savings. But, if we're not withdrawing from retirement funds, how else will we make ends meet?

Income and Expenses

We are in stabilization mode, maybe even survival mode. Where we can, we work to have a bit of financial slack so that we can breathe, change as necessary, and reinvent ourselves.[318]

We look for ways to generate more income, be it a second job or overtime at an existing job. We review where we can cut discretionary expenses—are we paying too much for cable or entertainment services? Is there a better phone plan? What can we use from the pantry or freezer and what substitutions can be made at the grocery store to trim food bills? We look for hidden pockets of savings, like available cash back on credit card accounts, and unused gift card balances. We ask for cash for birthdays and Christmas.

We may be able to save on interest expenses by consolidating some or all our debts. We may be able to adjust the minimum monthly student loan repayment. In some cases, we can limit our monthly payment to 10-20% of our discretionary income by talking with our lender and enlisting in an income-driven repayment plan. In some cases, we may be eligible for loan forgiveness, especially if we work as a teacher or in public service. Some lenders are willing to defer or pause our payments for a while. However, it is very important to work with our lenders because they have more power to affect our finances than most creditors due. For example, our much-needed tax refund could be taken and applied to the outstanding balance on our student loans if we are in default.

If we've paid ahead on our mortgage as suggested in Chapter 6, we may be able to renegotiate the terms of our mortgage. Paying ahead normally shortens the length of the note automatically. However, often lenders are amenable to keeping the original loan term and reducing the monthly payment instead.

We may consider bankruptcy. In the ideal, pre-bankruptcy, we would have thoughtfully structured our assets to include a substantial base of protected assets while maintaining sufficient liquidity to pay our bills. However, if we are in bankruptcy, we have some comfort in knowing that we may emerge from bankruptcy with some treasured assets.

Federal bankruptcy can discharge most of our debts if we are insolvent. In bankruptcy, all of our nonexempt assets become the property of the bankruptcy estate, and are sold or distributed to our creditors, with preferred creditors being paid first. We get to keep exempt assets even though we are in bankruptcy, and which assets are exempt are a matter of federal or state law. Exempt assets are generally only exposed to spouses and lienholders.[319] While states determine which assets are exempt, common exempt assets include the value of our home up to certain limits,[320] tools of our trade, life insurance policies, annuities, and retirement accounts. Some states have additional protections. For example, Delaware banking laws prohibit attachment or garnishment but the account must be only in Delaware which creates complications.[321] We might be able to protect our assets further through putting them in an LLC, but things get complicated very quickly, because the cost of such structuring may include losing popular homestead exemptions for property taxes and having to pay the mortgage in full due to the "due on sale" clauses in most mortgages. We might be able to protect some assets by transferring them to our spouse—if we trust our spouse. All these strategies are best undertaken with legal counsel.

We may file bankruptcy, but in some cases, creditors can force us into bankruptcy if we are sufficiently delinquent in our payments. Normally, there are three types of bankruptcy available to us as individuals—Chapter 7, Chapter 11, and Chapter 13. We file for bankruptcy in the state in which we have resided for the last two years. Chapter 7 bankruptcy is a total liquidation of our nonexempt assets as of a point in time. Any income earned after the filing date is ours, and unavailable to creditors.[322] Where our assets are sold for more than what is owed, we receive that excess. After the bankruptcy case is closed, we have a fresh start. Chapter 13 bankruptcy on the other hand is an opportunity to set a structured payment plan for all our creditors. If we can abide the agreed upon payment plan, we can keep our assets.[323] However, Chapter 13 availability has income caps—the wealthiest among us are not eligible.[324] Those of us above the caps, and those of us who own businesses may be able to file for Chapter 11 bankruptcy. At the end of bankruptcy, all our debts may be eliminated, regardless of how much of the debt was paid.

Small Businesses

If we own a business, another kind of bankruptcy, Chapter 11, may be available to us. Under Chapter 11, we retain possession of our assets and propose a repayment plan. Like Chapter 13, we keep the assets if we abide by an agreed upon repayment plan.

But, less drastic methods might also hold us over. For example, we may be able to sell or borrow against our Accounts Receivable. We may be able to consolidate or renegotiate our loans to reduce interest rates or borrow at a lower annual percentage rate to take advantage of purchase discounts. Purchase discounts may seem insignificant because of the language that we use to communicate them, but over the course of a year, they can be quite substantial. For example, terms on a purchase may be 2/10, n/30. When that happens, we can get a 2% discount if we pay within 10 days, or we can pay the whole amount within 30 days. Saving 2% for paying (30-10 =) 20 days early translates to (2%/ 20 days early x 365 days/year =) more than 36% annual percentage rate per year, which of course is quite a steep interest expense savings.

Do We Even Know How to Turn This Around?

A financial setback is a good time to reassess our lives. What is enough for us? So many luxuries are available to us even when we are not ultra-wealthy. We have good fresh food, access to medicine and health care, access to low-cost education, and entertainment. As Ben Casnocha said, "[t]oday, there's a tiny difference between the rich and the American middle class in terms of quality of life....what 'average' people in America share with the super rich(sic) Bill Gates is far more significant than what we don't share with him."[325] The quality of our relationships is more important. Having no meaningful relationships reduces our quality of life and being in poor quality relationships can be financially draining.

So What's Stopping Us?

As we get adjusted to one lifestyle, it's easy to lose touch with other lifestyle cultures, mindsets, and skill sets. We may need to replace current habits with older habits, at least temporarily. Below is a table summarizing transcendent strategies that can help remind us of the adjustments that we need to make to adjust to where we are and work toward where we wish to go, socioeconomically speaking.

A Summary of How to Move Up

Economic Status	Characterized by	Strategy to Succeed	Strategy to Transcend	Inherent Conflict	Lower Risk Tactics
Lower Low Class	When food is nearly exhausted	Everyone for themselves	Contract and cooperate to stabilize income	We're afraid that we will give more than we can take, especially when we have none to spare overall.	Enter into informal agreements carefully and monitor those that we contract with, with the goal of establishing trust.
Middle Low Class	Not starving, but homeless, or close to it	Get jobs with benefits like sick days. Form a social safety net.	Get a "regular job" with stable income and benefits. Contract our social network so that we're not lending money.	If we have a regular income, we're financing more people than are financing us, holding us back.	Split the difference. Only lend a portion (like up to half) out. That is, loving others as much, but only as much as we love ourselves.
Upper Low Class	Fed and housed, but with nothing left over	Get a "regular job" with stable income and benefits. Restrict lending out money.	Think longer term: lower our expenses over the course of a month or year, not day or week and develop skills to increase revenue. Save where we can, though maybe in useful assets like freezers and tools.	If we invest in assets to reduce costs over the longer term, we might need that money for an economic shock soon and have to borrow, sending us downward. Also, we may have to take on student loan debt to get a skill, leaving us with less net income to spend, not more.	Earmark an irregular gain, like tax return money for this type of investment. Study the income of the skills that a school is advertising very carefully: how many get jobs, and at what pay? Look closely at community colleges and inquire about grants and scholarships.
Lower Middle Class	Needs usually met, but vulnerable to economic shocks	Think longer term: control expenses and develop salable skills. Save regularly.	Need skills for managing debt & investing money in both traditional investment accounts like retirement accounts and choosing among less obvious investments like home ownership and education.	We need to control expenses because we make so little money, but we need to spend money to invest in skills that will make us more money. To do this, we may need to take on debt, but we also need to avoid debt because we can't afford the interest expense.	Start with research that costs no money. Carefully research the financial rewards of several different careers. Find a couple that pay. Carefully research the cost and time to get that training. Carefully research financial aid. Decide if there's a feasible plan to make more over the next 5-10 years.

Middle Middle Class	Financially independent of our family and friends and expect others to be the same. Uncomfortable discussing money.	Hold a steady job. Keep expenses & debt low. Accumulate assets for home and retirement.	Attain an upwardly mobile career. Manage debt and asset portfolio to maximize risk-adjusted return on investment over the longer term.	An upwardly mobile career might take money and time that could be used to earn overtime or maybe get earn a raise.	Carefully research the financial rewards of several different careers that use additional skills and the cost and time to get that training. Decide if there's a feasible plan to make more over the next 5–10 years. Be prepared to change employers once training is complete.
Upper Middle Class	Less focused on surviving, competing for success.	Succeed in our high paying careers, continuously looking for better jobs. Manage debt & expenses. Accumulate assets for wealth and retirement.	We need to manage our debt portfolio carefully and start an investment portfolio for short-, medium- and long-term goals.	To continue to grow takes time. We are tempted to take bigger risks rather than exercising patience. We need a trusted adviser to help us handle the complexity of life insurance, debt portfolios, retirement, and beginning investments.	Research current career and financial growth opportunities. Research cost and options for investment managers.
Lower Upper Class	We continue to compete for success. Some "fake it 'til we make it."	Increase our money skills. Spend less than what we make, saving for short- and long-term goals, and thoughtfully managing our debt.	Time and persistence are important. We have laid a strong financial foundation and need to maintain it. We need to obtain good financial advice from competent, trustworthy money managers, attorneys, and tax accountants. Income tax planning becomes a priority.	Having more money than is easily handled alone, but not knowing who we can trust or if paying them is worth the money.	Establish boundaries with family and friends. Hire professionals to assist with future growth of business goals. Continuously evaluate new opportunities for income growth and wealth.
Middle Upper Class	We've made it but we don't want anyone to know how much we have.	Manage our careers, businesses to increase income and wealth.	Carefully choose financial advisers and plan tax & wealth management with them.	Thinking that there is never enough money, even at the expense of important relationships. Thinking that we do not deserve our wealth.	Stay consistent with planning for and maintaining our wealth. Continuously evaluate new investments and opportunities.

CHAPTER 11

Conclusion

***"Wealth is the ability to fully experience life."*[326]**

To be financially successful and progress up the socioeconomic ranks, we need several resources, including time, ambition, education, professional connections, and some capital which to work. The balance of the elements shifts as we move up or down economic ranks. For example, when we're on the lower end of the economic scale, we are likely to have more time, but less money, and among our friends and neighbors, higher education may not be valued or may even be scorned and mocked. We also need to be able to adapt our own mindsets to the changing balance of resources, needs and financial rules of the climb, and that is probably not natural to us, because most people we know tend to hover within an economic step or two of where they were raised.

There are many self-help books and articles, but they are not always directed on a focused economic class. Taking otherwise good advice at the wrong place in the economic ladder can be futile or even damaging. And, some advice, while correct, is hard for us to take because of the then-correct lessons we've learned when we were at lower socioeconomic levels. Even when we correct our thought patterns and habits for a time, it's easy to revert to those former patterns that are hardwired in our brain. Fortunately, as we form new habits, they become hardwired as well, so resuming those habits is far easier than it was to learn them originally.

Managing our money is an emotionally fraught job that comes with a confusing vocabulary. Is it any wonder so many of us devote less time to personal finances than we do planning our next vacation? It is important to focus on building wealth, but more important to understand that finances are only part of wealth, and to understand the limitations that money has in our wealth portfolio. That is, building "wealth" isn't strictly about money, it's about finding the intersection between our life's purpose and the funds needed to achieve it. [327]

At the upper end of the scale, it's about meaning. So, even if we don't make the million, we still have a chance at the bigger, more meaningful life that can begin now. That doesn't mean that money is unimportant, but rather, that once we have enough, we have a choice whether to pursue more money, or pursue a higher purpose, or both. If we can't charter a private plane to Paris now, we can at least live like a millionaire now with respect to purpose. Adopt a rescue dog. Help teachers with supplies for their classes. Invest in spiritual healing. Serve the community.

We may find the meaning more satisfying than the extra money, which in part answers the question, "why isn't everyone a millionaire?"

Why Isn't Everyone a Millionaire?

The answer varies, and so should our financial strategies. Sometimes financial vulnerability is a symptom of an imbalanced life.

- Beverly[328] trusted the wrong people. She believed that others would always provide for her, but she outlived those who would.

She did not take personal responsibility for her own financial health.

- Ward and June saved for a comfortable retirement, but they were always a soft touch for spoiling their daughter and later her daughter's children. Drugs and legal problems exasperated the family dynamic. Ward and June just did not financially plan to raise two full families, and just did not insist that their daughter be financially responsible for herself or her family.

- Peter works hard, then spends his money on toys, or rather, down payments on toys. In addition to interest expense on toys like boats, RVs, ATVs, and frequent replacement of cars, he insures those toys, maintains those toys, and fills them with gas. They're fun for a while, but in the end, he doesn't have much time to play with them because he has to work harder to pay for them. He does not try to live beneath his means or control his hobby expenses.

- Dorothy is in a relationship with Joshua, who spends his money and hers.

- Elizabeth finds her low-income job frustrating and unfulfilling, so she quits but does not retool for a higher paying job. Without highly-demanded skills, she is left with few job choices. When she's working full-time, the benefits are often worth as much as the wages themselves. Often, only part-time jobs with no benefits are available. She does not have a plan to rise financially.

- Clint has anger management problems and jumps from job to job. Until his personal demons are faced, his financial ones will remain.

- Vicky hates debt, even when it can make her more money. Because she is emotional rather than rational about debt, her earnings grow much more slowly than they should.

- Cliff isn't a millionaire, but he's a millennial who is well on his way; if he stays the course, he will likely achieve that goal.

Sometimes financial vulnerability is a consequence of higher priorities.

- Opie is pursuing his dream job—it just doesn't pay very much or very regularly. With no children and no responsibilities other than supporting himself, he'd rather chase the dream now than wonder "what if" later.

- Mona had a child with special needs. She works enough to financially support her family, but all extra time is devoted to her child. She has more important things to do than to become a millionaire now.

- Lisa would rather change the lives of our youth than pursue money, so she teaches high school and throws herself into extracurricular activities that benefit the students.

Sometimes we do not have the financial education and skills specific to where we currently are to transcend, but education alone will not fix the problem. We need the discipline to consistently apply what we know. We need good habits. We need the social networks that support our rise. We need to overcome the fear of changing what were good, appropriate approaches to money as they become less useful and perhaps even hold us back. Moving through socioeconomic levels is partly rational and partly emotional. We balance these two elements financially and through the rest of our lives.

NOTES

1 Ward McAllister.

2 http://www.tvguide.com/galleries/bankrupt-celebrities-1080762/

3 http://www.msn.com/en-ca/sports/more-sports/21-sports-stars-whove-gone-bankrupt/ss-BBlmIiX

4 http://www.nytimes.com/2003/08/05/sports/tyson-s-bankruptcy-is-a-lesson-in-ways-to-squander-a-fortune.html?_r=0

5 The Notorious B.I.G.

6 http://money.cnn.com/2014/06/05/news/economy/how-much-income-to-be-happy/

7 http://money.cnn.com/2014/06/05/news/economy/how-much-income-to-be-happy/

8 Academic studies by Amos Tversky and Daniel Kahnemann call this "loss aversion." *Kahneman, D. & Tversky, A. (1979).* Prospect theory: An analysis of Decision under Risk. *Econometrica. 47(4): pages 263–291. doi:10.2307/1914185.*

9 Klontz, B., Britt, S.L., Mentzer, J. & Klontz, T. (2011). Money beliefs and financial behaviors: Development of the Klontz money script inventory. *The Journal of Financial Therapy,* 2(1): pages 1–22.

10 Tatzel, M. (2002). 'Money worlds' and well-being: An integration of money dispositions, materialism and price-related behavior. *Journal of Economic Psychology, 23*(1): pages 103–126.

11 Kasser, T., & Ahuvia, A. (2002). Materialistic values and well-being in business students. *European Journal of Social Psychology, 32*(1): pages 137–146.

12 Klontz, B., & Klontz, T. (2009). *Mind over money: Overcoming the money disorders that threaten our financial health.* Crown Business.

13 https://www.nytimes.com/2011/05/07/your-money/07wealth.html

14 1 Timothy 6:10.

15 http://time.com/4176128/powerball-jackpot-lottery-winners/

16 http://time.com/4176128/powerball-jackpot-lottery-winners/

17 Salary range column: https://www.visualcapitalist.com/household-income-100-homes/ Net worth to income: https://www.visualcapitalist.com/relationship-income-and-wealth/ Avg. net worth estimated as a 55-year-old individual: https://money.cnn.com/tools/networth ageincome/

https://www.visualcapitalist.com/14-percent-americans-negative-wealth/

18 Klontz,B., Britt, S.L., Mentzer, J. & Klontz, T. (2011). Money beliefs and financial behaviors: Development of the Klontz money script inventory. *The Journal of Financial Therapy, 2*(1): pages 1–22.

19 Kegan, R. and Lahey, L.L. (2009). *Immunity to change: How to overcome it and unlock the potential in yourself and your organization.* Harvard Business Review Press, Boston, MA.

20 The Hunger Games, Suzanne Collins.

21 Maslow, A. H. (1943). A theory of human motivation. *Psychological review, 50*(4): page 370.

22 Harlan Howard song "Busted," covered by Johnny Cash and Ray Charles, 1962.

23 Camerer, C., Babcock, L., Loewenstein, G., & Thaler, R. (1997). Labor supply of New York City cabdrivers: One day at a time. *Quarterly Journal of Economics,* 112 (May): pages 407–442.

24 Heath, C., & Soll, J. (1996). Mental accounting and consumer decisions. *Journal of Consumer Research,* 23 (1): pages 40–52.

25 Rizzo, J. & Zeckhauser, R. (2003). Reference incomes, loss aversion, and physician behavior. *The Review of Economics and Statistics,* 85 (4): pages 909–922.

26 Mullainathan, S., & Shafir, E. (2013). *Scarcity: Why having too little means so much.* Macmillan, page 36.

27 http://www.apa.org/monitor/2015/02/class-differences.aspx

28 Payne, R. K. (2013). *A framework for understanding poverty: A cognitive approach.* Highlands, TX: aha! Process.

29 http://www.marketwatch.com/story/more-than-35000-americans-reveal-their-biggest-financial-weakness-2016-07-20

30 Sapolsky, R. M. (2004). *Why zebras don't get ulcers: The acclaimed guide to stress, stress-related diseases, and coping-now revised and updated.* Holt paperbacks.

31 Mullainathan, S., & Shafir, E. (2013). *Scarcity: Why having too little means so much.* Macmillan, page 151.

32 Payne, R. K. (2013). *A framework for understanding poverty: A cognitive approach.* Highlands, TX: aha! Process, page 27.

33 Payne, R. K. (2013). *A framework for understanding poverty: A cognitive approach.* Highlands, TX: aha! Process, page 25.

34 http://www.marketwatch.com/story/more-than-35000-americans-reveal-their-biggest-financial-weakness-2016-07-20

35 Halpern-Meekin, S., Edin, K., Tach, L., & Sykes, J. (2015). *It's not like I'm poor: How working families make ends meet in a post-welfare world.* University of California Press, page 31.

36 Halpern-Meekin, S., Edin, K., Tach, L., & Sykes, J. (2015). *It's not like I'm poor: How working families make ends meet in a post-welfare world.* University of California Press.

37 Halpern-Meekin, S., Edin, K., Tach, L., & Sykes, J. (2015). *It's not like I'm poor: How working families make ends meet in a post-welfare world.* University of California Press, page 25.

38 Halpern-Meekin, S., Edin, K., Tach, L., & Sykes, J. (2015). *It's not like I'm poor: How working families make ends meet in a post-welfare world.* University of California Press.

39 Halpern-Meekin, S., Edin, K., Tach, L., & Sykes, J. (2015). *It's not like I'm poor: How working families make ends meet in a post-welfare world.* University of California Press.

40 Halpern-Meekin, S., Edin, K., Tach, L., & Sykes, J. (2015). *It's not like I'm poor: How working families make ends meet in a post-welfare world.* University of California Press.

41 http://healthland.time.com/2010/11/24/the-rich-are-different-more-money-less-empathy/#ixzz2pM2m29N3 January 21,2016.

42 https://www.northwesternmutual.com/life-and-money/how-managing-your-money-affects-your-brain/

43 Mullainathan, S., & Shafir, E. (2013). *Scarcity: Why having too little means so much.* Macmillan, page 107.

44 https://www.psychologytoday.com/blog/consumer-behavior/201303/five-reasons-we-impulse-buy

45 Drexler, A., Fischer, G. & Schoar, A. (2014). Keeping it simple: Financial literacy and rules of thumb. *American Economic Journal: Applied Economics, 6 (2).*

46 Mullainathan, S., & Shafir, E. (2013). *Scarcity: Why having too little means so much.* Macmillan, page 175.

47 Chambers, V. (2016). Lowering and raising tax withholding: do workers notice? *Business Studies Journal, 8(1):* pages 12–27.

48 Grandstaff, M. (2016). How our brains may be hard-wired against saving, *USA Today,* Oct. 27.

49 Thaler, R. H. (1999). Mental accounting matters. *Journal of Behavioral decision making, 12*(3), pages 183–206.

50 Thaler, R.H., & Sunstein, C.R. (2009). *Nudge: Improving decisions about health, wealth, and happiness.* Yale University Press, New Haven, CT.

51 Halpern-Meekin, S., Edin, K., Tach, L., & Sykes, J. (2015). *It's not like I'm poor: How working families make ends meet in a post-welfare world.* University of California Press, page 16.

52 Halpern-Meekin, S., Edin, K., Tach, L., & Sykes, J. (2015). *It's not like I'm poor: How working families make ends meet in a post-welfare world.* University of California Press, page 16.

53 Chambers, V. & Curatola, A. (2012). Could increasing the frequency of estimated tax payments increase compliance among the self-employed? *Advances in Taxation,* Dec., , *20*: pages 1–28. http://www.emeraldinsight. com/books.htm?issn=1058-7497&volume=20

54 Klontz, B., Britt, S.L., Mentzer, J. & Klontz, T. (2011). Money beliefs and financial behaviors: Development of the Klontz money script inventory. *The Journal of Financial Therapy, 2(1):* pages 1–22.

55 Winkelmann, R., Oswald, A. J., & Powdthavee, N. (2011, Aug.). What happens to people after winning the lottery. In *European Economic Association & Econometric Society Parallel Meetings,* pages 25–29.

56 Payne, R.K., DeVol, P. E., Smith, T.D. (2001). *Bridges out of Poverty.* Aha publishing, page 125.

57 Payne, R.K. (2013). *A framework for understanding poverty: A cognitive approach.* Highlands, TX: Aha! Process, page 26.

58 Mullainathan, S., & Shafir, E. (2013). *Scarcity: Why having too little means so much.* Macmillan, page 130.

59 Mullainathan, S., & Shafir, E. (2013). *Scarcity: Why having too little means so much.* Macmillan, page 130.

60 Mullainathan, S., & Shafir, E. (2013). *Scarcity: Why having too little means so much.* Macmillan, page 132..

61 Mischel, W., *Ebbesen, B., Raskoff Zeiss, A. (1972).* Cognitive and attentional mechanisms in delay of gratification. *Journal of Personality and Social Psychology.* 21 (2): pages 204–218. doi:10.1037/h0032198. *ISSN 0022-3514. PMID 5010404..*

62 Mullainathan, S., & Shafir, E. (2013). *Scarcity: Why having too little means so much.* Macmillan, page 82.

63 Mullainathan, S., & Shafir, E. (2013). *Scarcity: Why having too little means so much.* Macmillan, page 83.

64 Thompson, D. (2016). The two biases that keep people from saving money. *The Atlantic.* Jul. 17. http://www.theatlantic.com/business/archive/2016/07/two-biases/491576/

65 The *Wall Street Journal* estimated that 2/3 of U.S. employers offer no options for saving for retirement. http://blogs.wsj.com/economics/2015/09/29/the-biggest-reason-workers-dont-save-for-retirement/

66 Halpern-Meekin, S., Edin, K., Tach, L., & Sykes, J. (2015). *It's not like I'm poor: How working families make ends meet in a post-welfare world.* University of California Press, page 131.

67 This credit was enacted in 2001 for the 2002 tax year as Internal Revenue Code (IRC) Section 25B.

68 Chambers, V. (2015). Convenience may be necessary for wide-spread pension participation by the poor. *IRS Research Bulletin/U.S. Treasury, 2014*. http://www.irs.gov/pub/irs-soi/14rescon.pdf.

69 Run by the U.S. Treasury and launched in late 2015, employees could contribute to a safe, no fee retirement account that is guaranteed by the U.S. government to never lose value. We could sign up online and contribute as little as $2/month. Online applications showed what savings we can expect with small, regular contributions. For example, a contribution of $10/month for 20 years would yield a savings of over $3,109. This may have been by far the easiest, safest, most reliable retirement tool available for people in the lower U.S. economic levels. It was discontinued by the Trump administration in 2017.

70 See e.g. https://www.comptroller.texas.gov/taxes/publications/98-490/

71 Mullainathan, S., & Shafir, E. (2013). *Scarcity: Why having too little means so much*. Macmillan, page 94.

72 Mullainathan, S., & Shafir, E. (2013). *Scarcity: Why having too little means so much*. Macmillan, page 93.

73 Mullainathan, S., & Shafir, E. (2013). *Scarcity: Why having too little means so much*. Macmillan, page 104.

74 Mullainathan, S., & Shafir, E. (2013). *Scarcity: Why having too little means so much*. Macmillan, page 121.

75 Mullainathan, S., & Shafir, E. (2013). *Scarcity: Why having too little means so much*. Macmillan, page 60.

76 Mullainathan, S., & Shafir, E. (2013). *Scarcity: Why having too little means so much*. Macmillan, page 207.

77 Mullainathan, S., & Shafir, E. (2013). *Scarcity: Why having too little means so much*. Macmillan.

78 Thompson, D. (2016). The two biases that keep people from saving money. *The Atlantic*. Jul., page 17. http://www.theatlantic.com/business/archive/2016/07/two-biases/491576/

79 Sugar Ray Leonard, via Brainy quote at: https://www.brainyquote.com/quotes/sugar_ray_leonard_604802?src=t_middle-class

80 CNBC (2016). America's middle class is hollowing out in many cities. http://www.cnbc.com/2016/05/13/americas-middle-class-is-hollowing-out-in-many-cities.html

81 Kraus, M. W., Piff, P. K., Mendoza-Denton, R., Rheinschmidt, M. L., & Keltner, D. (2012). Social class, solipsism, and contextualism: how the rich are different from the poor. *Psychological Review, 119(3)*: page 546.

82 Kraus, M. W., Piff, P. K., Mendoza-Denton, R., Rheinschmidt, M. L., & Keltner, D. (2012). Social class, solipsism, and contextualism: how the rich are different from the poor. *Psychological Review, 119*(3): page 546.

83 Levenson, R. W., & Gottman, J. M. (1983). Marital interaction: physiological linkage and affective exchange. *Journal of Personality and Social Psychology*, 45(3): page 587.

84 Sawyer, J. (2014). *A tale of two psyches: Upper class vs. lower class psychology*. Summary of Talk .CUNY Graduate Center, http://www.stonybrook.edu/workingclass/images/2014conference_papers/sawyer.pdf

85 Stephens, N. M., Markus, H. R., & Townsend, S. S. (2007). Choice as an act of meaning: the case of social class. *Journal of Personality and Social Psychology*, *93*(5): page 814. See also: Weininger, E. B., & Lareau, A. (2009). Paradoxical pathways: An ethnographic extension of Kohn's findings on class and childrearing. *Journal of Marriage and Family*, *71*(3): pages 680–695.

86 Piff, P. K., Kraus, M. W., Côté, S., Cheng, B. H., & Keltner, D. (2010). Having less, giving more: the influence of social class on prosocial behavior. *Journal of Personality and Social Psychology*, *99*(5), page 771.

87 Mullainathan, S., & Shafir, E. (2013). *Scarcity: Why having too little means so much*. Macmillan, page 160.

88 Dalio, R. (2017). Our biggest economic, social, and political issue: The top 40% and the bottom 60%. https://www.linkedin.com/pulse/our-biggest-economic-social-political-issue-two-economies-ray-dalio/

89 http://www.marketwatch.com/story/more-than-35000-americans-reveal-their-biggest-financial-weakness-2016-07-20

90 http://www.marketwatch.com/story/more-than-35000-americans-reveal-their-biggest-financial-weakness-2016-07-20 .

91 http://www.marketwatch.com/story/more-than-35000-americans-reveal-their-biggest-financial-weakness-2016-07-20.

92 Mullainathan, S., & Shafir, E. (2013). *Scarcity: Why having too little means so much*. Macmillan, page 50.

93 Dalio, R. (2017). Our biggest economic, social, and political issue: The top 40% and the bottom 60%. https://www.linkedin.com/pulse/our-biggest-economic-social-political-issue-two-economies-ray-dalio/

94 https://www.mcclatchydc.com/news/politics-government/article24538864.html

95 Sawyer, J. (2014). *A tale of two psyches: Upper class vs. lower class psychology*. Summary of Talk .CUNY Graduate Center, http://www.stonybrook.edu/workingclass/images/2014conference_papers/sawyer.pdf; see also Piff, P. K., Kraus, M. W., Côté, S., Cheng, B. H., & Keltner, D. (2010). Having less, giving more: the influence of social class on prosocial behavior. *Journal of Personality and Social Psychology*, *99*(5), page 771.

96 Mullainathan, S., & Shafir, E. (2013). *Scarcity: Why having too little means so much*. Macmillan, pages 117–118.

9797 Payne, R. K. (2013). *A framework for understanding poverty: A cognitive approach*. Highlands, TX: aha! Process, page 113.

98 Mullainathan, S., & Shafir, E. (2013). *Scarcity: Why having too little means so much*. Macmillan, page 212.

99 Mullainathan, S., & Shafir, E. (2013). *Scarcity: Why having too little means so much*. Macmillan, page 221.

100 Varnum, M.E.W. (2015). Higher in status, (even) better-than-average. *Frontiers in Psychology*, 6: page 496. http://doi.org/10.3389/fpsyg.2015.00496

101 Children who were poor at age nine had greater amygdala activity and lower prefrontal cortex activity at age 24. They showed patterns of dysregulation of emotions in dealing with stress and threats people with Post-Traumatic Stress Disorder, depression, anxiety disorders, and aggression. Sawyer, J. (2014). *A tale of two psyches: Upper class vs. lower class psychology*. Summary of Talk .CUNY Graduate Center, http://www.stonybrook.edu/workingclass/images/2014conference_papers/sawyer.pdf,

102 The poor have about 10 distinct financial instruments on average. Collins, D., Morduch, J., Rutherford, S., & Ruthven, O. (2010). *Portfolios of the poor: how the world's poor live on $2 a day*. Princeton University Press, page 233.

103 https://www.360financialliteracy.org/Get-Started?ftp=1

104 www.prosperitynow.org.

105 Dalio, R. (2017). Our biggest economic, social, and political issue: The top 40% and the bottom 60%. https://www.linkedin.com/pulse/our-biggest-economic-social-political-issue-two-economies-ray-dalio/

106 http://www.economist.com/blogs/graphicdetail/2013/05/daily-chart-0 1.21.2016

107 Stevenson B. & Wolfers J. (2008). *Economic growth and subjective well-being: Reassessing the Easterlin paradox*. Brookings Paper Econ Activ 2008 (Spring): pages 1–87.

108 DeAngelis, T. (2004). Consumerism and its discontents. *Monitor on Psychology*. Mischel, W., Ebbesen, E. B., & Raskoff Zeiss, A. (1972). Cognitive and attentional mechanisms in delay of gratification. *Journal of Personality and Social Psychology*, *21*(2), page 204. http://www.apa.org/monitor/jun04/discontents.aspx.

109 DeAngelis, T. (2004). Consumerism and its discontents. *Monitor on Psychology*. Mischel, W., Ebbesen, E. B., & Raskoff Zeiss, A. (1972). Cognitive and attentional mechanisms in delay of gratification. *Journal of Personality and Social Psychology*, *21*(2), page 204. http://www.apa.org/monitor/jun04/discontents.aspx

110 DeAngelis, T. (2004). Consumerism and its discontents. *Monitor on Psychology*. Mischel, W., Ebbesen, E. B., & Raskoff Zeiss, A. (1972). Cognitive and attentional mechanisms in delay of gratification. *Journal of Personality and Social Psychology*, *21*(2), page 204. http://www.apa.org/monitor/jun04/discontents.aspx

111 DeAngelis, T. (2004). Consumerism and its discontents. *Monitor on Psychology*. Mischel, W., Ebbesen, E. B., & Raskoff Zeiss, A. (1972). Cognitive and attentional mechanisms in delay of gratification. *Journal of Personality and Social Psychology*, *21*(2), page 204. http://www.apa.org/monitor/jun04/discontents.aspx

112 DeAngelis, T. (2004). Consumerism and its discontents. *Monitor on Psychology*. Mischel, W., Ebbesen, E. B., & Raskoff Zeiss, A. (1972). Cognitive and attentional mechanisms in delay of gratification. *Journal of Personality and Social Psychology*, *21*(2), page 204. http://www.apa.org/monitor/jun04/discontents.aspx

113 DeAngelis, T. (2004). Consumerism and its discontents. *Monitor on Psychology*. Mischel, W., Ebbesen, E. B., & Raskoff Zeiss, A. (1972). Cognitive and attentional mechanisms in delay of gratification. *Journal of Personality and Social Psychology*, *21*(2), page 204. http://www.apa.org/monitor/jun04/discontents.aspx

114 No author (2016). Taking the pain out of payday loans, *Consumer Reports*, page 8.

115 No author (2016). Taking the pain out of payday loans, *Consumer Reports*, page 8.

116 Mullainathan, S., & Shafir, E. (2013). *Scarcity: Why having too little means so much*. Macmillan, page 115.

117 http://www.nerdwallet.com/blog/credit-card-data/average-credit-card-debt-household/

118 Mullainathan, S., & Shafir, E. (2013). *Scarcity: Why having too little means so much*. Macmillan, page 118.

119 Chambers, V. & Curatola, A. (2012). Could increasing the frequency of estimated tax payments increase compliance among the self-employed? *Advances in Taxation*, Dec., , *20*: pages 1–28. http://www.emeraldinsight.com/books.htm?issn=1058-7497&volume=20.

120 Duflo, E. & National Bureau of Economic Research. (2005). *Saving incentives for low- and middle-income families: Evidence from a field experiment with H & R Block*. Cambridge, Mass: National Bureau of Economic Research.

121 Payne, R.K., DeVol, P. E., Smith, T.D. (2001). *Bridges out of Poverty*, Aha publishing, page 147.

122 https://www.nytimes.com/2017/02/09/upshot/a-secret-of-many-urban-20-somethings-their-parents-help-with-the-rent.html

123 Benartzi, S., & Thaler, R. (2007). Heuristics and biases in retirement savings behavior. *Journal of Economic Perspectives*, *21*(3): pages 81–104.

124 Madrian, B. C., & Shea, D. F. (2001). The power of suggestion: Inertia in 401(k) participation and savings behavior. *The Quarterly journal of economics*, *116*(4), pages 1149–1187. See also Choi, J. J., Laibson, D., Madrian, B. C., & Metrick, A. (2005). Saving for retirement on the path of least resistance. *Rodney L White Center for Financial Research-Working Papers*, *9*; and Choi, J. J., Laibson, D., Madrian, B. C., & Metrick, A. (2002). Defined contribution pensions: Plan rules, participant choices, and the path of least resistance. *Tax Policy and the Economy*, *16*, pages 67–113.

125 Madrian, B. C., & Shea, D. F. (2001). The power of suggestion: Inertia in 401(k) participation and savings behavior. *The Quarterly journal of economics*, *116*(4), pages 1149–1187.

126 Bodie, Z., & Prast, H. (2012). Rational pensions for irrational people, behavioral science lessons for the Netherlands. *The Future of Multi-Pillar Pensions*, pages 299–329.

127 https://www.debt.org/2014/02/28/cfpb-sues-itt/

128 Orson Welles, via https://www.brainyquote.com/quotes/orson_welles_539020?src=t_middle-class

129 http://www.cnbc.com/2016/05/13/americas-middle-class-is-hollowing-out-in-many-cities.html

130 Cohen, P. (2015). Middle class, but feeling economically insecure. *New York Times*. Apr. 11.

131 http://www.huffingtonpost.com/2013/05/15/redefining-success-americ_n_3279718.html

132 https://static.cdn.responsys.net/i2/responsysimages/content/valic/vc22976SavingsMatters-072016.pdf

133 Dalio, R. (2017). Our biggest economic, social, and political issue: The top 40% and the bottom 60%. https://www.linkedin.com/pulse/our-biggest-economic-social-political-issue-two-economies-ray-dalio/

134 https://www.psychologytoday.com/blog/psychology-yesterday/201610/the-psychology-being-middle-class

135 Cohen, P. (2015). Middle class but feeling economically insecure. *New York Times*. Apr. 11.

136 Dalio, R. (2017). Our biggest economic, social, and political issue: The top 40% and the bottom 60%. https://www.linkedin.com/pulse/our-biggest-economic-social-political-issue-two-economies-ray-dalio/

137 Dalio, R. (2017). Our biggest economic, social, and political issue: The top 40% and the bottom 60%. https://www.linkedin.com/pulse/our-biggest-economic-social-political-issue-two-economies-ray-dalio/

138 Dalio, R. (2017). Our biggest economic, social, and political issue: The top 40% and the bottom 60%. https://www.linkedin.com/pulse/our-biggest-economic-social-political-issue-two-economies-ray-dalio/

139 https://www.bls.gov/oes/current/oes_nat.htm

140 *https://fafsa.ed.gov/*

141 www.irsvideos.gov/Businesses

142 https://www.sba.gov/offices/headquarters/oee

143 Drexler, A., Fischer, G. & Schoar, A. (2014). Keeping it simple: Financial literacy and rules of thumb. *American Economic Journal: Applied Economics, 6 (2),* pages 1–31. In this article, the authors find that simple rules of thumb, of progressing sophistication are very useful for micro-entrepreneurs. The easiest rules of thumb were presented in the last chapter. The rules in this chapter build upon those first steps.

144 Halpern-Meekin, S., Edin, K., Tach, L., & Sykes, J. (2015). *It's not like I'm poor: How working families make ends meet in a post-welfare world.* University of California Press, page 174.

145 Halpern-Meekin, S., Edin, K., Tach, L., & Sykes, J. (2015). *It's not like I'm poor: How working families make ends meet in a post-welfare world.* University of California Press, page 174.

146 There's a growing percentage who are too discouraged to apply for credit despite needing it. The differences https://www.marketwatch.com/story/one-third-of-americans-say-theyd-have-trouble-coming-up-with-an-emergency-2000-2017-03-20 were most pronounced by credit score—only 11% of those with a credit score of 760 and above said they would have difficulty, versus 64% of those with a credit score of 680 and below.

147 Halpern-Meekin, S., Edin, K., Tach, L., & Sykes, J. (2015). *It's not like I'm poor: How working families make ends meet in a post-welfare world.* University of California Press, page 179.

148 Halpern-Meekin, S., Edin, K., Tach, L., & Sykes, J. (2015). *It's not like I'm poor: How working families make ends meet in a post-welfare world.* University of California Press, page 176-179.

149 Halpern-Meekin, S., Edin, K., Tach, L., & Sykes, J. (2015). *It's not like I'm poor: How working families make ends meet in a post-welfare world.* University of California Press, page 178.

150 Halpern-Meekin, S., Edin, K., Tach, L., & Sykes, J. (2015). *It's not like I'm poor: How working families make ends meet in a post-welfare world.* University of California Press, page 176-179.

151 One survey found the share of respondents who were too discouraged to apply is rising. There's a growing percentage who are too discouraged to apply for credit despite needing it. https://www.marketwatch.com/story/one-third-of-americans-say-theyd-have-trouble-coming-up-with-an-emergency-2000-2017-03-20

152 *Immunity to Change* is the inspiration for this section of each chapter. Kegan, R., & Lahey, L. L. (2009). *Immunity to change: How to overcome it and unlock potential in yourself and your organization.* Harvard Business Press.

153 http://www.theatlantic.com/business/archive/2016/07/two-biases/491576/

154 http://www.theatlantic.com/business/archive/2016/07/two-biases/491576/

155 George Bailey, *It's a Wonderful Life*

156 Samuel, L. R. (2016). The psychology of being middle class: Why do almost all Americans think they're part of the middle class? *Psychology Yesterday* Posted Oct. 6.

157 Payne, R. K. (2013). *A framework for understanding poverty: A cognitive approach.* Highlands, TX: Aha! Process, page 32.

158 Macculloch, R., Di Tella, R., Oswald, A.J. (2001). Macroeconomics of happiness. *Review of Economics and Statistics. 85(4)*, DOI 10.2139/ssrn.285918

159 Payne, R. K. (2013). *A framework for understanding poverty: A cognitive approach.* Highlands, TX: Aha! Process, page 44.

160 Cohen, P. (2015). Middle class but feeling economically insecure. *New York Times.* Apr. 11.

161 There's a growing percentage who are too discouraged to apply for credit despite needing it. https://www.marketwatch.com/story/one-third-of-americans-say-theyd-have-trouble-coming-up-with-an-emergency-2000-2017-03-20

162 https://money.usnews.com/investing/articles/2016-09-14/how-to-save-for-retirement-while-paying-for-a-childs-college

163 Chambers, V., & Spencer, M. (2009). All I know about money I learned in Kindergarten: The piggy bank system of decision-making. *Income Taxes: Policies, Rates and Effects.* Nova Science Publishers, Inc. ISBN 978-1-60741-626-5.

164 https://www.usatoday.com/story/money/personalfinance/retirement/2017/02/07/how-much-do-you-need-fund-retirement-more-than-you-think/96784474/

165 https://www.usatoday.com/story/money/personalfinance/retirement/2017/02/07/how-much-do-you-need-fund-retirement-more-than-you-think/96784474/

166 Not all bonds are safe; some default. Unsecured bonds are roughly as safe as the issuer of the bonds is financially sound. Secured bonds sound like they are safer than unsecured bonds but are only as safe as the underlying security. For example, if a bond is secured by the income from a project that is to be constructed and that project is subsequently not constructed, the bond issuer may well default and we lose our investment. If the bonds are secured by cattle and the bond issuer defaults, we might receive cattle in lieu of cash.

167 https://money.usnews.com/money/personal-finance/earning/articles/2017-02-10/phased-retirement-the-next-big-trend

168 "529" refers to the Internal Revenue Code section that authorizes the exclusion from income of interest, dividends, capital gains and other returns on the principal of this type of account.

169 See Texas Education Code §54.341, Hazlewood Act statute.

170 Dickler, J. (2017). Student Loan Balances Jump Nearly 150 Percent in a Decade. CNBC.com. 29 Aug.

171 https://www.cnbc.com/video/2017/05/30/how-to-deal-with-college-debt.html

172 See the Tax Cuts and Jobs Act of 2017 (Public Law 115–97) and IRC Sec. 163(h)(3)(F) as amended by Act Sec. 11043(a) and subsequent U.S. Treasury Regulations.

173 Chambers, V., & Spencer, M. (2008). Does changing the timing of a yearly individual tax refund change the amount spent vs. saved? *Journal of Economic Psychology*, *29*(6): pages 856–862.

174 Hsieh, C. T. (2003). Do consumers react to anticipated income changes? Evidence from the Alaska permanent fund. *American Economic Review*, *93*(1): pages 397–405, page 397.

175 Browning and Collado (2001) studied Spanish panel data to measure the effect of the bonus payments customary in that market. Workers in this bonus paying scheme usually received payments of 1/14th of their annual wage per month for 10 months. However, in two months, usually December and June or July, they received bonuses of 2/14ths of their salary. They "do not find any effect of anticipated changes in income on expenditure patterns over the year for those who receive the bonus payments are indistinguishable from the patterns of those who do not receive a bonus," (Browning, M., & Collado, M. D. (2001). The response of expenditures to anticipated income changes: panel data estimates. *American Economic Review*, *91*(3): page 682).

176 http://www.nerdwallet.com/blog/credit-card-data/average-credit-card-debt-household/

177 http://www.nerdwallet.com/blog/credit-card-data/average-credit-card-debt-household/

178 http://www.nerdwallet.com/blog/credit-card-data/average-credit-card-debt-household/

179 http://www.nerdwallet.com/blog/credit-card-data/average-credit-card-debt-household/

180 http://www.nerdwallet.com/blog/credit-card-data/average-credit-card-debt-household/

181 http://www.nerdwallet.com/blog/credit-card-data/average-credit-card-debt-household/

182 Fitzgerald, M. A., Haynes, G. W., Schrank, H. L., & Danes, S. M. (2010). Socially responsible processes of small family business owners: Exploratory evidence from the national family business survey. *Journal of Small Business Management*, *48*(4): pages 524–551; Madden, K., Scaife, W., & Crissman, K. (2006). How and why small to medium size enterprises (SMEs) engage with their communities: An Australian study. *International Journal of Nonprofit and Voluntary Sector Marketing*, *11*(1): pages 49–60; Feliu, N., & Botero, I. C. (2016). Philanthropy in family enterprises: A review of literature. *Family Business Review*, *29*(1): pages 121–141.

183 http://www.nerdwallet.com/blog/credit-card-data/average-credit-card-debt-household/

184 Forster, G.A. (2013). *Asset Protection for Professionals, Entrepreneurs and Investors.* Aspire Publishing, LLC.

185 Wallflowers, *One Headlight*

186 Mullainathan, S., & Shafir, E. (2013). *Scarcity: Why having too little means so much.* Macmillan, pages 132–133.

187 Mullainathan, S., & Shafir, E. (2013). *Scarcity: Why having too little means so much*. Macmillan, page 137.

188 Theme from *The Jeffersons*.

189 Kahneman, D., & Deaton, A. (2010). High income improves evaluation of life but not emotional well-being. *Proceedings of the National Academy of Sciences, 107*(38).

190 Payne, R. K. (2013). *A framework for understanding poverty: A cognitive approach*. Highlands, TX: aha! Process, page 57.

191 http://time.com/money/4991215/upper-middle-class-characteristics/

192 http://time.com/money/4991215/upper-middle-class-characteristics/

193 https://www.psychologytoday.com/blog/psychology-yesterday/201610/the-psychology-being-middle-class

194 For an example of an application of mental accounting as it pertains to retirement, see: https://www.usatoday.com/story/money/personalfinance/retirement/2017/04/05/try-mental-accounting-make-your-retirement-dreams-come-true/99321350/

195 https://www.linkedin.com/pulse/our-biggest-economic-social-political-issue-two-economies-ray-dalio/

196 https://www.linkedin.com/pulse/our-biggest-economic-social-political-issue-two-economies-ray-dalio/

197 http://www.bloomberg.com/news/articles/2016-09-20/make-six-figures-there-s-a-decent-chance-you-ve-got-almost-nothing-in-the-bank

198 Loewenstein, G. (1987). Anticipation and the valuation of delayed consumption. *The Economic Journal, 97* (387): pages 666–684.

199 Parker, J. A. (1999). The reaction of household consumption to predictable changes in social security taxes. *American Economic Review, 89* (4): pages 959–973.

200 https://www.nytimes.com/2017/04/26/business/calculating-college-savings-needs.html

201 https://www.cnbc.com/2017/08/29/student-loan-balances-jump-nearly-150-percent-in-a-decade.html

202 Loans that defer the accrual of interest on the student loans on graduation are preferred because of the interest expense savings.

203 https://www.forbes.com/sites/elainepofeldt/2013/02/26/many-firms-dont-bounce-back-after-owners-die/#1535c5f2247b

204 Rozen, C. (2018). Succession Plan Top Concern at CPA Firms, as Baby Boomers Retire, *Accounting Policy & Practice Report. https://www.bna.com/succession-plan-top-n73014477533/*

205 See the homestead laws for your state.

206 An opportunity cost is the benefit from Choice 1 that we miss out on when we choose Choice 2.

207 Payne, R. K. (2013). *A framework for understanding poverty: A cognitive approach.* Highlands, TX: aha! Process, page 53.

208 Payne, R. K. (2013). *A framework for understanding poverty: A cognitive approach.* Highlands, TX: aha! Process, page 56.

209 *All the Right Moves*, One Republic.

210 Adler, N. E., Boyce, T., Chesney, M. A., Cohen, S., Folkman, S., Kahn, R. L., & Syme, S. L. (1994). Socioeconomic status and health: the challenge of the gradient. *American Psychologist, 49* (1): page 15. See also Kawachi, I., Kennedy, B. P., Lochner, K., & Prothrow-Stith, D. (1997). Social capital, income inequality, and mortality. *American Journal of Public Health, 87* (9): pages 1491–1498.

211 Chambers, V., Spencer, M. K., & Mollick, J. S. (2009). Goldilocks Rebates: Complying with Government Wishes Only When Rebate Amount Is" Just Right". *Journal of Economics and Economic Education Research, 10* (1): page 101.

212 https://www.bloomberg.com/news/articles/2018-05-03/america-is-minting-more-millionaire-retirees-than-ever

213 Young, C., Varner, C., Lurie, I. Z., & Prisinzano, R. (2016). Millionaire migration and taxation of the elite: Evidence from administrative data. *American Sociological Review, 81* (3): pages 421–446.

214 About 2.2% of the time, rich people move for tax reasons, and then they generally move to Florida, leaving little impact on tax revenues in the states they leave behind. Young, C., Varner, C., Lurie, I. Z., & Prisinzano, R. (2016). Millionaire migration and taxation of the elite: Evidence from administrative data. *American Sociological Review, 81* (3): pages 421–446.

215 Dunn, E. W., Gilbert, D. T., & Wilson, T. D. (2011). If money doesn't make you happy, then you probably aren't spending it right. *Journal of Consumer Psychology, 21* (2): pages 115–125.

216 See http://www.360financialliteracy.org/Topics/Investor-Education/Sudden-Wealth/Could-You-Handle-a-Financial-Windfall; Diener, E., & Seligman, M. E. (2004). Beyond money: Toward an economy of well-being. *Psychological Science in the Public Interest, 5* (1): pages 1–31. See also Nisslé, S., & Bschor, T. (2002). Winning the jackpot and depression: Money cannot buy happiness. *International Journal of Psychiatry in Clinical Practice, 6* (3): pages 183–186.

217 Brickman, P., Coates, D., & Janoff-Bulman, R. (1978). Lottery winners and accident victims: Is happiness relative? *Journal of Personality and Social Psychology, 36* (8): page 917.

218 https://www.irs.gov/irm/part5/irm_05-021-002

219 The Kiplinger Tax Letter, 91 (8), April 22, 2016.

220 See also articles such as: http://www.360financialliteracy.org/Topics/Investor-Education/Sudden-Wealth/When-I-play-the-lottery-I-have-to-choose-between-a-lump-sum-and-annual-payments.-Does-it-matter

221 For a detailed legal analysis, see Forster, G.A. (2013) *Asset Protection for Professionals, Entrepreneurs and Investors.* Aspire Publishing, LLC.

222 https://www.nolo.com/legal-encyclopedia/prenuptial-agreements-overview-29569.html

223 Moody, M., Lugo Knapp, A., & Corrado, M. (2011). What is a family foundation?. *The Foundation Review, 3* (4): page 5.

224 Forster, G.A. (2013). *Asset Protection for Professionals, Entrepreneurs and Investors.* Aspire Publishing, LLC.

225 Forster, G.A. (2013). *Asset Protection for Professionals, Entrepreneurs and Investors.* Aspire Publishing, LLC.

226 Forster, G.A. (2013). *Asset Protection for Professionals, Entrepreneurs and Investors.* Aspire Publishing, LLC.

227 https://www.journalofaccountancy.com/newsletters/2017/apr/avoid-inheritance- mistakes.html?utm_source=mnl:cpald&utm_medium=email&utm_campaign=06Apr2017

228 https://www.journalofaccountancy.com/newsletters/2017/apr/avoid-inheritance-mistakes.html?utm_source=mnl:cpald&utm_medium=email&utm_campaign=06Apr2017

229 https://www.cnbc.com/2016/10/21/6-mental-tricks-rich-people-use-to-make-more-money.html

230 Woolley, S. (2018). America Is Minting More Millionaire Retirees Than Ever, *Bloomberg*, May 3. https://www.bloomberg.com/news/articles/2018-05-03/america-is-minting-more-millionaire-retirees-than-ever

231 Woolley, S. (2018). America Is Minting More Millionaire Retirees Than Ever, *Bloomberg*, May 3. https://www.bloomberg.com/news/articles/2018-05-03/america-is-minting-more-millionaire-retirees-than-ever

232 Portnoy, B. (2018). *The Geometry of Wealth: How to shape a life of money and meaning.* Harriman House Limited.

233 http://www.huffingtonpost.com/2014/01/06/psychology-of-wealth_n_4531905.html

234 See for example the fundraisers promoted by the Florida Institute of CPAs Scholarship Foundation.

235 Facebook exec Sean Parker's character famously quipped in the movie The Social Network. Fincher, D., Sorkin, A., Mezrich, B., Eisenberg, J., Garfield, A. and Timberlake, J. (2016). *The Social Network (2010).* [online] IMDb. Available at: http://www.imdb.com/title/tt1285016/ [Accessed 22 Jun. 2016].

236 https://psmag.com/five-studies-the-psychology-of-the-ultra-rich-according-to-the-research-fffab386ae6f#.54ofomycm

237 https://psmag.com/five-studies-the-psychology-of-the-ultra-rich-according-to-the-research-fffab386ae6f#.54ofomycm

238 Frank, R. (2008). *Richistan: A journey through the American wealth boom and the lives of the new rich.* Crown Business, page 3.

239 Casnocha, B. (2016). https://www.linkedin.com/pulse/pros-cons-being-super-rich-ben-casnocha, Published on Apr. 14.

240 https://psmag.com/five-studies-the-psychology-of-the-ultra-rich-according-to-the-research-fffab386ae6f#.54ofomycm

241 https://psmag.com/five-studies-the-psychology-of-the-ultra-rich-according-to-the-research-fffab386ae6f#.54ofomycm

242 Kraus, M. W., & Keltner, D. (2013). Social class rank, essentialism, and punitive judgment. *Journal of Personality and Social Psychology, 105* (2): page 247.

243 Casnocha, B. (2016). https://www.linkedin.com/pulse/pros-cons-being-super-rich-ben-casnocha, Published on Apr. 14.

244 http://www.stonybrook.edu/workingclass/images/2014conference papers/sawyer.pdf, A Tale of Two Psyches: Upper Class vs. Lower Class Psychology, Jeremy Sawyer, CUNY Graduate Center, Summary of Talk

245 Payne, R. K. (2013). *A framework for understanding poverty: A cognitive approach*. Highlands, TX: aha! Process, page 45.

246 Princeton Survey Research Associates International for Pew & American Association for the Advancement of Science, June 2009 as cited in https://www.scribd.com/document/225509828/The-American-Majority-Is-A-Populist-Majority#

247 https://www.merriam-webster.com/dictionary/noblesse%20oblige

248 http://www.huffingtonpost.com/2014/01/06/psychology-of-wealth_n_4531905.html; see also Piff, P. K., Kraus, M. W., Côté, S., Cheng, B. H., & Keltner, D. (2010). Having less, giving more: the influence of social class on prosocial behavior. *Journal of Personality and Social Psychology, 99* (5): pages 771.

249 Piff, P. K. (2014). Wealth and the inflated self: Class, entitlement, and narcissism. *Personality and Social Psychology Bulletin, 40* (1): pages 34–43.

250 See Robert Hare's research, e.g. Babiak, P., & Hare, R. D. (2007). *Snakes in suits*. HarperCollins. See also: Sawyer, J. (2014). *A tale of two psyches: Upper class vs. lower class psychology*. Summary of Talk .CUNY Graduate Center, http://www.stonybrook.edu/workingclass/images/2014conference_papers/sawyer.pdf

251 http://www.huffingtonpost.com/2014/01/06/psychology-of-wealth_n_4531905.html; See also Van Kleef, G. A., Oveis, C., Van Der Löwe, I., LuoKogan, A., Goetz, J., & Keltner, D. (2008). Power, distress, and compassion: Turning a blind eye to the suffering of others. *Psychological Science, 19* (12): pages 1315–1322.

252 http://www.huffingtonpost.com/2014/01/06/psychology-of-wealth_n_4531905.html

253 Piff, P. K. (2014). Wealth and the inflated self: Class, entitlement, and narcissism. *Personality and Social Psychology Bulletin, 40* (1): pages 34–43.

254 http://www.huffingtonpost.com/2014/01/06/psychology-of-wealth_n_4531905.html; see also Piff, P. K., Kraus, M. W., Côté, S., Cheng, B. H., & Keltner, D. (2010). Having less, giving more: the

influence of social class on prosocial behavior. *Journal of Personality and Social Psychology, 99* (5): page 771.

255 Frank, R. (2008). *Richistan: A journey through the American wealth boom and the lives of the new rich.* Crown Business, **page 76.**

256 https://www.nytimes.com/2006/07/02/business/yourmoney/02view. html

257 http://theweek.com/articles/597963/brief-history-billionaire-philanthropists-people-who-hate

258 Andrew Carnegie wrote "The Gospel of Wealth," an 1889 article that became a guiding philosophy for philanthropists.

259 https://www.uh.edu/engines/epi177.htm

260 Kraus, M. W., Chen, S., & Keltner, D. (2011). The power to be me: Power elevates self-concept consistency and authenticity. *Journal of Experimental Social Psychology, 47* (5): pages 974–980.

261 Piff, P. K. (2014). Wealth and the inflated self: Class, entitlement, and narcissism. *Personality and Social Psychology Bulletin, 40* (1): pages 34–43.

262 https://www.merriam-webster.com/dictionary/affluenza

263 http://www.huffingtonpost.com/2014/01/06/psychology-of-wealth_n_4531905.html

264 http://www.huffingtonpost.com/2014/01/06/psychology-of-wealth_n_4531905.html

265 http://www.huffingtonpost.com/2014/01/06/psychology-of-wealth_n_4531905.html

266 Woolley, S. (2018). America Is Minting More Millionaire Retirees Than Ever, *Bloomberg,* May 3. https://www.bloomberg.com/news/articles/2018-05-03/america-is-minting-more-millionaire-retirees-than-ever "The gap between the wealthy and the ultra-wealthy has also widened. The wealth of the median millionaire rose by about 12 percent

from 1989 to 2016, while the median millionaire's equity position was swelling from 27 percent of financial accounts to 55 percent. The wealth of the top 1 percent of millionaires, meanwhile, more than doubled, from $14.9 million to $31.3 million, in 2016 dollars, as their equity positions jumped from 30 percent to 69 percent, according to the report."

267 https://psmag.com/five-studies-the-psychology-of-the-ultra-rich-according-to-the-research-fffab386ae6f#.54ofomycm

268 Casnocha, B. (2016). https://www.linkedin.com/pulse/pros-cons-being-super-rich-ben-casnocha, Published on Apr. 14.

269 "Provenance" is a record of ownership that is used to authenticate that the item is not a forgery or fake "knockoff."

270 https://psmag.com/five-studies-the-psychology-of-the-ultra-rich-according-to-the-research-fffab386ae6f#.54ofomycm

271 Feliu, N., & Botero, I. C. (2016). Philanthropy in family enterprises: A review of literature. *Family Business Review*, *29* (1): pages 121–141.

272 Campopiano, G., De Massis, A., & Chirico, F. (2014). Firm philanthropy in small-and medium-sized family firms: The effects of family involvement in ownership and management. *Family Business Review*, *27* (3): pages 244–258.

273 Cruz, C., Larraza–Kintana, M., Garcés–Galdeano, L., & Berrone, P. (2014). Are family firms really more socially responsible?. *Entrepreneurship Theory and Practice*, *38* (6): pages 1295–1316.

274 Feliu, N., & Botero, I. C. (2016). Philanthropy in family enterprises: A review of literature. *Family Business Review*, *29* (1): pages 121–141.

275 Feliu, N., & Botero, I. C. (2016). Philanthropy in family enterprises: A review of literature. *Family Business Review*, *29* (1): pages 121–141.

276 Donnelly, G. E., Zheng, T., Haisley, E., & Norton, M. I. (2018). The Amount and Source of Millionaires' Wealth (Moderately) Predict Their Happiness. *Personality and Social Psychology Bulletin*, 0146167217744766.

277 Donnelly, G. E., Zheng, T., Haisley, E., & Norton, M. I. (2018). The Amount and Source of Millionaires' Wealth (Moderately) Predict Their Happiness. *Personality and Social Psychology Bulletin*, 0146167217744766.

278 Donnelly, G. E., Zheng, T., Haisley, E., & Norton, M. I. (2018). The Amount and Source of Millionaires' Wealth (Moderately) Predict Their Happiness. *Personality and Social Psychology Bulletin*, 0146167217744766.

279 Donnelly, G. E., Zheng, T., Haisley, E., & Norton, M. I. (2018). The Amount and Source of Millionaires' Wealth (Moderately) Predict Their Happiness. *Personality and Social Psychology Bulletin*, 0146167217744766.

280 Donnelly, G. E., Zheng, T., Haisley, E., & Norton, M. I. (2018). The Amount and Source of Millionaires' Wealth (Moderately) Predict Their Happiness. *Personality and Social Psychology Bulletin*, 0146167217744766.

281 Forster, G.A. (2013). *Asset Protection for Professionals, Entrepreneurs and Investors*. Aspire Publishing, LLC., page 154.

282 https://www.cnbc.com/2017/07/06/billionaires-who-wont-leave-their-fortunes-to-their-kids.html

283 Examples include FaceBook founder Mark Zuckerberg and wife Priscilla Chan who founded the Chan Zuckerberg Initiative, an LLC dedicated to "personalized learning, curing disease, connecting people, and building strong communities" worldwide, Warren Buffett and Bill and Melinda Gates, all of whom are leaving a substantial amount to the Bill and Melinda Gates foundation, and Andrew Lloyd Webber and Michael Bloomberg. https://www.cnbc.com/2017/07/06/billionaires-who-wont-leave-their-fortunes-to-their-kids.html

284 Bill Gates, to "This Morning" last year, as reported by SFGate. https://www.cnbc.com/2017/07/06/billionaires-who-wont-leave-their-fortunes-to-their-kids.html

285 https://www.cnbc.com/2017/07/06/billionaires-who-wont-leave-their-fortunes-to-their-kids.html

286 https://www.cnbc.com/2017/07/06/billionaires-who-wont-leave-their-fortunes-to-their-kids.html

287 Portnoy, B. (2018). *The Geometry of Wealth: How to shape a life of money and meaning*. Harriman House Limited.

288 Portnoy, B. (2018). *The Geometry of Wealth: How to shape a life of money and meaning*. Harriman House Limited.

289 Mark Twain.

290 The names in this section have been changed or are composites of several people

291 Dalio, R. (2017). Our biggest economic, social, and political issue: The top 40% and the bottom 60%. https://www.linkedin.com/pulse/our-biggest-economic-social-political-issue-two-economies-ray-dalio/

292 Cohen, P. (2015). Middle class but feeling economically insecure. *New York Times*. Apr. 11.

293 Cohen, P. (2015). Middle class but feeling economically insecure. *New York Times*. Apr. 11.

294 Cohen, P. (2015). Middle class but feeling economically insecure. *New York Times*. Apr. 11.

295 Jimmy Buffett (1983). One Particular Harbour.

296 https://www.usatoday.com/story/money/2017/02/14/you-have-2-choices-reduce-spending-now-scale-back-retirement-lifestyle/97719232/. Paul Davidson, USA TODAY Published 9:26 a.m. ET Feb. 14, 2017 | Updated 2:23 p.m. ET Feb. 14, 2017. Portnoy, B. (2018). *The Geometry of Wealth: How to shape a life of money and meaning*. Harriman House Limited.

297 Mullainathan, S., & Shafir, E. (2013). *Scarcity: Why having too little means so much*. Macmillan, page 137.

298 Mullainathan, S., & Shafir, E. (2013). *Scarcity: Why having too little means so much*. Macmillan, page 229. One societal effect of being poor is that while unemployment climbs, so does quality of decisions. Not that stress is always bad: stress produced by deadlines, for example can

be good. Groups with tighter deadlines were more productive. They also reported being happier, page 23.

299 Payne, R. K. (2013). *A framework for understanding poverty: A cognitive approach*. Highlands, TX: Aha! Process, page 61.

300 Kübler-Ross, E. (1969) *On Death and Dying*, Routledge. ISBN 0-415-04015-9

301 Payne, R. K. (2013). *A framework for understanding poverty: A cognitive approach*. Highlands, TX: Aha! Process, pages 94–95.

302 http://www.huffingtonpost.com/2014/01/06/psychology-of-wealth_n_4531905.html

303 Johnny Paycheck, *Take This Job and Shove It*.

304 https://www.usatoday.com/story/money/2017/02/14/you-have-2-choices-reduce-spending-now-scale-back-retirement-lifestyle/97719232/ Paul Davidson, USA TODAY Published 9:26 a.m. ET Feb. 14, 2017 Updated 2:23 p.m. ET Feb. 14, 2017.

305 Davidson, P. (2017). *USA Today*. Feb. 14. https://www.usatoday.com/story/money/2017/02/14/you-have-2-choices-reduce-spending-now-scale-back-retirement-lifestyle/97719232/

306 https://www.journalofaccountancy.com/news/2017/apr/americans-fear-they-wont-reach-retirement-goals-201716417.html?utm_source=mnl:cpald&utm_medium=email&utm_campaign=12Apr2017 By Samiha Khanna. In that same poll, only 5% of the over 1,000 people surveyed had already reached their financial retirement goal.

307 O'Brien, S. (2017). *CNBC*. Aug. 2017. https://www.cnbc.com/2017/08/18/pre-retirement-financial-jitters-heres-what-to-do.html.

308 Powell, R. (2017). Try mental accounting to make your retirement dreams come true. *USA Today*. Apr. 5.

309 Buck Owens & Roy Clark, *Gloom, Despair and Agony on Me*.

310 https://money.usnews.com/investing/articles/2016-09-14/how-to-save-for-retirement-while-paying-for-a-childs-college

311 https://money.usnews.com/investing/articles/2016-09-14/how-to-save-for-retirement-while-paying-for-a-childs-college

312 Tella, R. D., MacCulloch, R. J., & Oswald, A. J. (2003). The macroeconomics of happiness. *Review of Economics and Statistics, 85* (4): pages 809–827.

313 Kadlec, D. (2017). *Money.* June 19. http://time.com/money/4820854/retirement-income-saving-job-loss/ . In the study led by Teresa Ghilarducci, an income shock was defined as at least a 10% decline in pay "as a result of something like a job change, job loss, or ill health.

314 Tella, R. D., MacCulloch, R. J., & Oswald, A. J. (2003). The macroeconomics of happiness. *Review of Economics and Statistics, 85* (4): pages 809–827.

315 Mullainathan, S., & Shafir, E. (2013). *Scarcity: Why having too little means so much.* Macmillan, page 207.

316 Kadlec, D. (2017). *Money.* June 19. http://time.com/money/4820854/retirement-income-saving-job-loss/. One 10% setback typically results in almost $1,200 less savings in retirement, whereas chronic health problems can reduce retirement savings by $34,500–$86,300 on average. People who lost all income for a year drained retirement savings by an average of $6,218.

317 Kadlec, D. (2017). *Money.* June 19. http://time.com/money/4820854/retirement-income-saving-job-loss/

318 Mullainathan, S., & Shafir, E. (2013). *Scarcity: Why having too little means so much.* Macmillan, Note 187, page 207.

319 Forster, G.A. (2013). *Asset Protection for Professionals, Entrepreneurs and Investors.* Aspire Publishing, LLC.

320 For an excellent discussion and 50-state table of homestead exemptions, see: Forster, G.A. (2013). *Asset Protection for Professionals, Entrepreneurs and Investors.* Aspire Publishing, LLC.

321 Forster, G.A. (2013). *Asset Protection for Professionals, Entrepreneurs and Investors.* Aspire Publishing, LLC.

322 Forster, G.A. (2013). *Asset Protection for Professionals, Entrepreneurs and Investors.* Aspire Publishing, LLC.

323 Forster, G.A. (2013). *Asset Protection for Professionals, Entrepreneurs and Investors.* Aspire Publishing, LLC.

324 As of 2013, the debt limits for Chapter 13 were $360,475 for unsecured debts and $1,081,000 in secured debts. Forster, G.A. (2013). *Asset Protection for Professionals, Entrepreneurs and Investors.* Aspire Publishing, LLC.

325 Casnocha, B. (2016). https://www.linkedin.com/pulse/pros-cons-being-super-rich-ben-casnocha, Published on Apr. 14.

326 Henry David Thoreau.

327 Portnoy, B. (2018). *The Geometry of Wealth: How to shape a life of money and meaning.* Harriman House Limited.

328 In these cases, either the names have been changed, or the cases are composites of several people.